weekendLearning
Series

# Islamic Studies

## Level 2

Mansur Ahmad and Husain A. Nuri

ISBN:  978-1-936569-58-8

First edition:    2008
Second edition:  2009
Third edition:    2010
Fourth edition:   2012
Reprint:         2013, 2014, 2016
Revised and enlarged edition: 2018
Reprint:         2019, 2020

Cover Design and Photography:  Mansur Ahmad
Illustrations: Abira Das, Husain Nuri, Mansur Ahmad

Weekend Learning Publishers
5584 Boulder Crest St.
Columbus, OH 43235, USA
www.weekendlearning.com

Printed in India

# Preface

The concept of a series of Islamic Studies books was conceived in 2002 when both of us were teachers or principals of two weekend schools in two different states. We used several excellent textbooks and reference books for the schools. However, as educators we soon realized there was no single textbook available that could meet our classroom needs. Some of the available books had too many or too few lessons for an academic year. Some lessons were too long for a class hour, and some were too short. Some lessons were too difficult for the student's age or too basic for higher-level classes. Some books were written without a 12-year curriculum in mind. The lessons in higher grades, therefore, did not develop from the knowledge base of prior years. Sometimes extra emphasis was placed on one topic at the expense of other important topics. Thus, we thought a balanced knowledge base was lost.

We always felt there ought to be a way out. We began writing the lessons ourselves to meet the needs of our schools. We involved other teachers. For the next two years, we conducted classes based on the lessons we prepared. In the meantime, both of us met other principals and teachers across the country. We wanted to find out how they taught Islamic Studies and what their major concerns were. Most of the principals and teachers we talked to, expressed their inability to find or develop a good curriculum. If they had a curriculum, they could not find lessons to complement the curriculum.

This survey prompted us to develop a functional, comprehensive curriculum for weekend schools in the West. We wanted to have a curriculum that would include everything that Muslim students growing up in the West would ideally need to know. We wanted to include topics based on the life experiences of students growing up in the West. Muslim children growing up in the US, Europe and Australia are facing diverse challenges and conflicting pressures at schools and in friend circles. They are constantly influenced by the mainstream youth culture. We wanted lessons to address their issues from their perspective.

The curriculum alone would not be of any use unless there were lessons based on the curriculum. The lessons had to be age appropriate, and suitable for the typical class duration of most of the schools. As we continued to write and edit lessons over the next two years, we made the curriculum increasingly meaningful.

In 2007, we published pre-printed coil bound versions of these books. More than thirty schools in the US and UK used the books. We also received a large number of inquiries from many other schools. Based on the suggestions, comments and reviews received from many of these schools, we have edited the books and made changes as appropriate.

We are thankful to Allāhﷻ for giving us the ability to write these books. We pray to Allāhﷻ to accept our labor and make us successful in communicating the message of Islam. We hope Islamic schools and home schools in the USA and other countries will find these books useful. Any mistakes or errors in the books are our fault. We appreciate receiving meaningful comments and suggestions to improve the series.

رَبَّنَا تَقَبَّلْ مِنَّا إِنَّكَ أَنتَ السَّمِيعُ الْعَلِيمُ ۝

*"Our Rabb! Accept from us, you indeed are the all-Hearing, all-Knowing."* (2:127)

Columbus
January 15, 2008

Mansur Ahmad
Husain A. Nuri

# Preface to the Revised and Enlarged Edition

All praise is due to Allāh﷾ alone. We are indebted to Him for giving us time, energy, and resources to publish this book and other books in this series. The first edition of the book was published in 2008. Over the next 10 years, we made small editorial changes in some of the lessons. During this time, our books became one of the most-sought-after series all over the world for teaching Islam in weekend schools. Thousands of schools on all the continents adopted our series, and we are indebted to the teachers, students, and above all, to almighty God.

We do not want to remain stagnant with the success of the series. We have been constantly striving to improve the books to meet the changing and growing needs of the weekend schools. Some teachers wrote to us requesting additional material in some of the lessons. In view of their requests, we have revised and enlarged all the lessons, adding more information and resources. Our utmost focus all along has been to remain extremely loyal and true to the teachings of the Qur'ān and authentic sunnah of the Messengerﷺ. With the enlarged lessons, teachers are now equipped with more materials while keeping the teaching time in class the same. We believe that the additional material and the new way of presenting information will enrich the classes, reduce the burden on teachers, and improve the overall learning experience.

We are grateful to Brenda Rusch for editing and proofreading this book and other books in this series. She has not only eliminated some grammatical, punctuation, and spelling errors, but she also improved content flow, transitions, and overall organization. Even after all corrections, some errors inadvertently remained. Thanks to Farzana Rahman and Nazar Maaf, they read the book all over again and corrected those that we missed. May Allāh﷾ accept our small effort.

June 15, 2018

Husain A. Nuri
Mansur Ahmad

# Table of Contents

## Unit 4: Learning About Islam

## Unit 5: Akhlaq and Adab in Islam

## Appendix

# How to use this book effectively
# Instructions for teachers and parents

Each lesson in this grade starts with a coloring or an activity page. The purpose of this page is to help students to compose themselves before the lesson begins. Students should be given about 5-10 minutes to complete the coloring activity. A word of appreciation or encouragement, insha-Allāh, will improve the attention of the class. If the teacher sits close to students, and at a similar height to the chairs of students, he or she might be able to command more attention. Please avoid monotonous voice; rather change the sound of the voice from normal speaking to whispering as appropriate. Use body languages, such as, use your hands to show a flying bird when teaching "Allah created all the birds." Be creative in teaching! Make frequent eye contact with the students. Ask questions frequently to reinforce learning.

For maximum benefit, each lesson should be completed within one class time. We recommend that a test be conducted every fifth or sixth lesson. For this and other books in this series, an Annotated Teacher's Edition is available. The Teacher's Edition has teaching ideas, lesson plans and other details that might benefit teachers.

## Homework:

Teachers are requested to assign and grade homework regularly. The time commitment for homework is about 10–15 minutes per lesson. Parents are strongly encouraged to supervise the student during the homework. Regular supervision of homework by a parent will indicate that education is valued.

## Teaching Respect:

From an early age, students should be taught to show respect to Allāh, His Messengers, Angels and the Companions. The teachers and parents are requested to mention the following:

- Whenever the word Allāh appears in the book, please add the glorification "*Subhāna-hu wa-Ta'ālā.*"
- Whenever the word Muhammad, or other words indicating Muhammad, e.g. Rasulullah, the Prophet, or Nabi appears, please add the prayer, "*Salla-llāhu 'alaihi wa Sallam.*" We have used in the book to remind the prayer.
- Whenever the student comes across the names of a prophet or an angel, please add the prayer "*Alai-hi-s Salām.*" This is noted by (A).
- For the first grade, this book does not introduce the Khalifahs and the Sahabahs. However, the students should be taught to add the prayer "*Radi-allāhu 'an-hu*" for a khalifa or a male companion of the Nabi. For a lady companion, the prayer "*Radi-allāhu 'an-hā*" should be used.

## Suggestions:

Please provide suggestions, corrections, ideas, etc., to improve the book by sending an e-mail to the publisher at info@weekendLearningl.com. It is a combined effort of the publisher, authors, teachers and parents to prepare our future ummah. May Allāh guide us all! Amin.

# Unit 1: The Creator and His Message

The objective of the unit is to introduce Allah﷾ to students. There is so much to learn about our Creator that volumes could be written, yet we will remain brief. Students come to school with very little knowledge of Allah﷾—what does He do and what does He not do. How does He create? These questions seem simple, yet the answers reveal profound information. Two chapters on the Qur'an and Hadith and Sunnah attempt to introduce these important areas of learning. The goal here is to keep it simple and enjoyable, yet informative. If students learn just the basic information presented in each chapter, then that will suffice. The concepts introduced here are vast, and they will be discussed in greater detail in future grades.

Lesson 1:      Allah﷾: *Our Creator*

Lesson 2:      How Does Allah﷾ Create?

Lesson 3:      What Does Allah﷾ Do?

Lesson 4:      Allah﷾: What Does He Not Do?

Lesson 5:      The Qur'ān

Lesson 6:      Hadith and Sunnah

# Unit 1: The Creator and His Message

## Allah: *Our Creator*

Who is Allāh, what and how did He create? Students will learn some essential, but basic facts about Allāh. This introductory lesson prepares students to take necessary step in a structured curriculum in a formal learning environment.

## How Does Allah Create?

It seems simple to say Allāh creates. But the mechanism and uniqueness of creations is elaborate and precise. Students will learn some of the mechanisms to understand that Allāh's creation is not similar to the way we make things. We cannot create. The lesson emphasizes this point in a easy-to-understand manner.

## What Does Allah Do?

Students learned that Allāh creates. What else does He do? Once we try to understand many other areas of divine action, we will get a better realization of our Creator. The things that Allāh does for us has profound impact on our survival. This lesson explores many of the things that Allāh does for us.

## Allah: What Does He Not Do?

Allāh being most-Powerful, He could do anything He wants to do. There is no doubt about it. But He does not do many things. He does not do many things that we do on a routine basis. Understanding of this point will help students know more about our Creator.

## The Qur'ān

After learning about Allāh in the next step, students will learn about divine guidance. Students are now introduced to the Qur'ān—the book of guidance. The students will learn some of the basics of the Qur'ān. Who sent it? How long did it take to finish the Qur'ān? What does it have? What are some of its specialties? The lesson answers these questions in simple and easy to understand language.

## Hadith and Sunnah

Children often hear about Hadith and Sunnah. This lesson explains them the fundamental difference between Hadith and Sunnah. Why do we follow these? Who collected the Hadith? These basic questions are answered in this final chapter of the Unit 1.

# Allah ﷾: *Our Creator*

Assalamu alaikum. Welcome to the class. Let us begin by coloring this Arabic word. The word is **Allah**.

## Subhanahu wa ta'āla

Allah **subhanahu wa ta'āla** is our creator. The word "subhanahu wa ta'āla" means "**Glory** to Him, the High." It is common practice in Islam that we say or write a word of glory after Allah's name. There are many words of glory. In this book, we will say "subhanahu wa ta'āla" to honor Him. We use it to show our respect. In English, we write (**swt**) to remind us to say "subhanahu wa ta'āla." In this book, we will use the following Arabic word of glory.

### Subhanahu Wa Ta'āla

## Allah﷾ is our creator

Allah﷾ is the Creator. He created the heavens and the earth. If you look at the sky on a clear night, you will see thousands of stars. Allah﷾ created all of them.

Allah﷾ created everything for a reason. He created many things to help us. For example, Allah﷾ created the sun to help us. Without the sun, nothing in the world could live and grow. Allah﷾ created day and night. We work during the day and sleep at night. Allah﷾ created air for us. Without clean air to breathe, we could not live even for a minute. Allah﷾ created water for us. We need water every day. Our bodies are even made of water.

## Allah ﷻ creates in pairs

Allah ﷻ created everything in the best way. He created living things in **pairs**. A pair means two things that are alike.

Allah ﷻ created many types of living things. There are so many types of insects, birds, fish, plants, fruits, and vegetables. Allah ﷻ created elephants and giant dinosaurs. When you see a butterfly, remember that it was created by Allah ﷻ. Only Allah ﷻ can create. Nobody else can create. Some people worship **idols**, but idols cannot create anything.

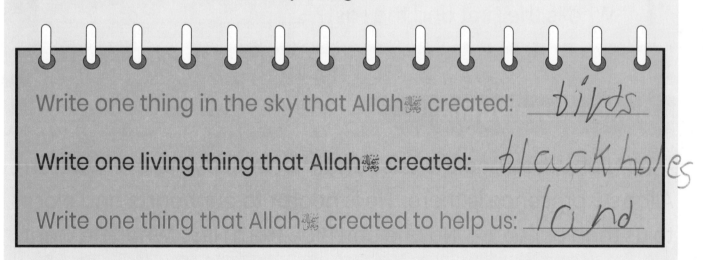

Write one thing in the sky that Allah ﷻ created: _birds_

Write one living thing that Allah ﷻ created: _black holes_

Write one thing that Allah ﷻ created to help us: _land_

## Countless creations

We could never finish counting all of Allah's creations. Even if we had thousands of pens, we could not write all the things that Allah created.

## The First and the Last

You might wonder: Where was Allah before the earth, planets, and sky were created?

Allah was always there. Long before the earth and the sky were created Allah was there. Long after the earth and the sky are destroyed, Allah will still be there. For this reason, we say Allah is the **First** and He is also the **Last**.

Can we finish counting Allah's creations? __no__

How many things did the idols create? __Zero__

Who is the First and the Last? __Allah swt__

## Owner of **everything**

To Allah belongs the East and the West. Wherever we turn, Allah's presence is there. He is nearer to our hearts and closer to us than our **veins**. No one can hide from Him. When He wants to create something, He says, "Be," and it becomes. Such is His power.

## No help is needed

A school has many teachers. One teacher cannot teach all the classes. A store has many sales people. One salesperson cannot run a store. An office has many people working in it.

The earth is very large. There are many thousands of animals, birds and other **creatures** on the earth. The sky is huge. There are thousands of stars in the sky.

How does Allah﷾ manage everything that He created? Does He need help? Does He have **partners** who help Him? The answer is **No**. Allah﷾ has no partners. Allah says:

لَا شَرِيكَ لَهُ

## La sharika lahu

It means: **He has no partners**.

Allah manages everything on His own. Allah is the one and only. Therefore, He does not need other gods or partners to help Him. Actually, there are no other gods but Allah.

### A look at nature

Everything we see in nature was created by Allah. He created the birds, trees, grass, colorful flowers, fruits, and vegetables. Allah also created rocks and sand. The next time you see a river or a mountain, think about who made it.

On your way home today, look out your car windows. See how many things Allah made in this world. We should remember to thank Him for everything He has created for us.

**Words that I learned today:**
Subhanahu Wa Ta'āla • Glory • (swt) • Pair • Idol
Veins • Creatures • Partners • La Sharika Lahu

1. Write four things that Allahﷻ created in the ovals below.

Universe

Air

carbiohe de oxside

humans

2. Fill in the blanks with the correct word from the box below.

create    everything    pairs    veins    thank you

Allahﷻ creates things in ___pairs___.

We should always say ___thank you___ to Allahﷻ.

Allahﷻ created ___everything___.

Allahﷻ is closer to us than our ___veins___.

Idols cannot ___create___ anything.

3. Who is our Creator?

___Allah swt___

4. Draw a picture of something that Allahﷻ created inside the box.

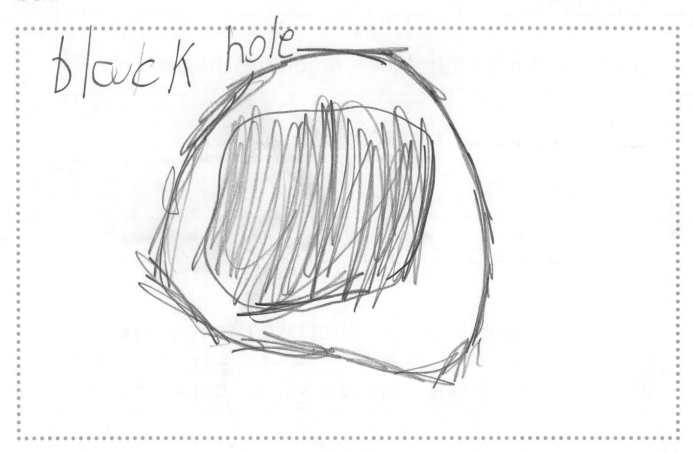

black hole

5. Everything that we can make comes from something that Allahﷻ gave us. Circle only the things that we can make using something Allahﷻ created.

Rain    House    Mountains    Cars    Sun

Horse    Stars    Playground    Trees    Grass

Pencil    Flower    Books    Apple    River

6. How many partners helped Allah﷾ when He created the stars and planets?

    A. Two partners

    B. Five partners

    C. No partners.

7. What is the meaning of the phrase, "La Sharika Lahu?"

    A. Allah﷾ is most-Merciful.

    B. Allah﷾ has no partners.

    C. Allah﷾ is the First and the Last.

8. Allah﷾ says He is closer to us than one of our body organs. Which organ is mentioned in the lesson?

    A. Veins

    B. Stomach

    C. Brain

# How Does Allah﷾ Create?

Assalamu alaikum. Welcome to the class. Allahﷻ creates the mountains, the clouds and everything else out of nothing. Only Allahﷻ can create in this way. Let us color the picture.

## Allah﷾ is al-Khaliq

We have learned that Allahﷻ creates. One of His beautiful names is **al-Khaliq**. It means "the Creator."

ٱلْخَـٰلِقُ

**Al-Khaliq**

This name also indicates that Allahﷻ creates with a plan. He creates using proper **measurements** and **proportions**.

## We only make things

How do we make things? We make small things like pens, crayons and toys. We also make large things like buildings, cars and ships.

Does this mean we are creators? No, we are not creators. We simply **make** things. We need plastic to make toys. We need wood and nails to make houses. We need metal and glass to make cars or ships. We cannot make anything if the **basic materials** are not available. Plastic, wood, and metal are some basic materials. Someone makes the basic materials, and then we use them to make other things.

## We can only make

When Allah﷾ decides to create something, He creates out of nothing. He does not wait for someone to make the basic materials for Him. When Allah﷾ decided to create the earth, He created it. When He decided to create the soil, oceans, air and other things, He created them. He creates when nothing exists. Even now, Allah﷾ is still creating many things.

## No help is needed

We cannot make many things just by ourselves. We need help from others to make a house, a playground, furniture, and other things.  The larger the item, the more people are required. After working for a while, we feel tired.  Then we take a break. Allah﷾ does not need help from anybody to create. He creates everything on His own. He does not get tired of creating. He does not need to rest.

## Varieties in creation

Allah ﷻ creates everything in **varieties**. There are millions of varieties of plants, animals, and flowers. Apples have about 7,500 varieties. Roses have about 150 varieties. Fish have about 15,000 varieties. Clouds have various types and shapes. There are different kinds of mountains. The oceans, seas, lakes, and rivers have various shapes and types of water.

No two human beings are exactly the same. There are many varieties in human beings, too.

## Proper measurement

When we make something, it is important that we use proper **measurements** and **proportions**. Imagine what could happen if we use too much salt, oil, or spices during cooking.

Imagine someone makes a pair of sneakers that are too odd to wear. Everything we use in our lives needs to be properly measured and proportioned.

Allah﷾ makes everything in its proper proportion and measurement. Elephants are large for a reason. Mosquitoes are small for a reason. Our hands, eyes, ears, and every part of our body is in proper proportion to the rest of our bodies.

## "Be" and it becomes

When Allah﷾ wants to create something, He simply says "**Be,**" and it becomes.

Allah﷾ says He created the sky and the earth with a special command. He said, "Be," and they were created. Such is Allah's﷾ power. He did not require help from anybody. He did not require any basic materials to create.

Everything in the universe was created with the order "Be." Even human beings were created with this order.

## Pairs in creation

Allah﷾ has a wonderful method of creation. Allah﷾ says He creates everything in **pairs**. A pair means two things that are very similar.

In the animal world, we can easily see these pairs. The pairs are males and females. For example, a **rooster** and a hen. A cow and a bull. A lion and a lioness.

In the plant world, we cannot easily see a male and female pair. But there are pairs. A male tree will not grow fruit. Only female trees grow fruit.

A pair does not always mean a male and female. Allah﷾ says in every type of creation, there are two kinds. A few examples of these pairs are day and night; winter and summer; rain and snow; hills and mountains; stars and planets; and the sun and the moon.

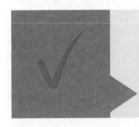

**Words that I learned today:**
Khaliq • Basic materials • Varieties • Be
Measurement • Proportion • Pair • Rooster

1. What is the meaning of the word Khaliq?

   A. Protector

   B. Provider

   C. Creator

2. Which choice is correct about Allah'sﷻ creations?

   A. He creates in varieties.

   B. He creates with the help of partners.

   C. He waits for someone to make the basic materials.

3. What can happen if proper measurements and proportions are not used when we make something?

_____

_____

3. Unscramble the following letters to make meaningful words.

**S A B C I**    b a s i c

**P R A I**    p a i r

4. Write YES if the sentence is correct. Write NO if it is not correct.

Allah﷾ needs basic materials to create.  _No_

Allah﷾ creates everything in large varieties.  _yes_

After making many varieties of things, Allah﷾ needs some rest.  _No_

Allah﷾ says "be" and nothing happens.  _No_

5. Fill in the blanks with the correct word from the box below.

| basic | be | measurement | more | pairs |

Plants and animals have _pairs_ in them.

Allah﷾ created the sky and the earth with a special command _be_.

Everything we use in our lives, needs proper _measurement_

When we make something, the larger the item, the _more_ people are required.

We cannot make anything if the _basic_ materials are not available.

# What Does Allahﷻ Do?

Assalamu alaikum. Welcome to the class. Let us begin by coloring the fly. Allahﷻ created flies and all living things. Nobody else can create. Only Allahﷻ can create.

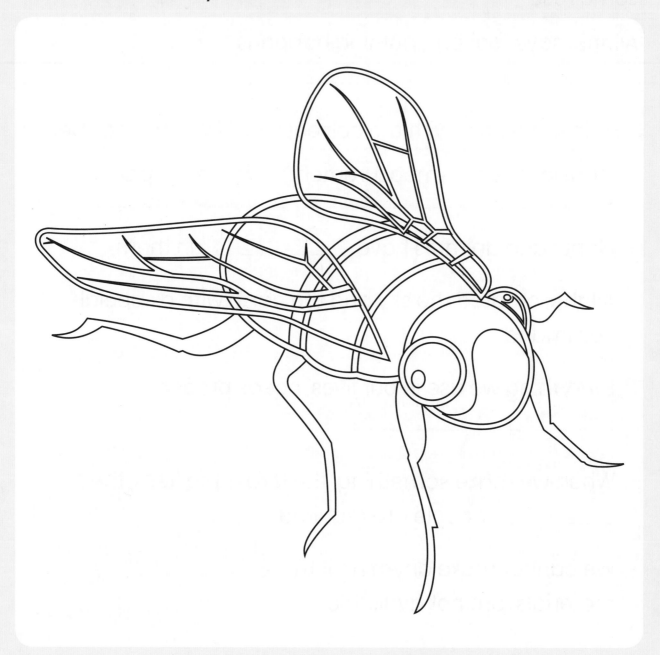

## Allah does it better

Allah has many beautiful names. Many of these names tell us things that He does. Whatever He does, He does it much better than any of us. He also does many things that we cannot do. This is because Allah is most Powerful. One of His most beautiful names is **al-Aziz**. It means the Mighty, or the Powerful.

**Al-Aziz**

## Allah creates

We already learned that Allah creates. We learned that Allah creates animals, plants and flowers. He also created the sun, the moon, and everything on the earth.

Can we create a single bird or a single tree? Can we create a sun or a Moon? No, we cannot create anything.

A housefly is a very small fly. We cannot even create a fly.

## Creates and perfects

Not only does Allahﷻ create, He also makes His creation **perfect**. To make something perfect means to make it in the best way. It also means to make it complete. For example, Allahﷻ would not create a fly without wings, a bird without feathers, or a dog without legs. Whatever is needed for a fly or a bird to become perfect, Allahﷻ gives it. There are no **defects** in His creation.

## Allahﷻ loves us

We learned that Allahﷻ is the **owner** of everything on earth and in the sky. He is the owner because He created them. He **loves** His creations. Allahﷻ loves us. Our parents also love us. But Allahﷻ loves us even more than our parents do.

Allahﷻ loves us so much that He gives His **blessings** to everybody. People who do not believe in Allahﷻ still get some blessings. Those who believe in Him get many more blessings. Allahﷻ gives us many gifts. Let us learn about some of these gifts.

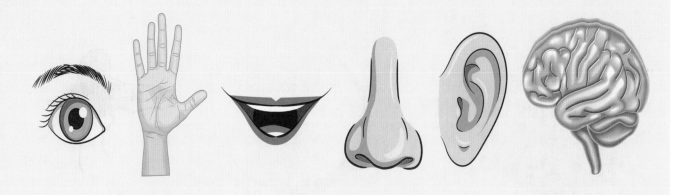

Let us think about our heads. Allahﷻ gave us two eyes, so we can see. Eyes are wonderful gifts from Allahﷻ. He gave us a nose, so we can smell. He gave us ears, so we can hear. He gave us skin, so we can feel. He also gave us a brain, so we can think. These are all gifts from Allahﷻ. These gifts are His blessings to us.

## Allahﷻ forgives, guides

If we make a mistake and ask Allahﷻ to **forgive** us, He will forgive us. Allahﷻ always wants us to be good people. He **guides** us so that we do not make mistakes in our lives. Allahﷻ guides us to be good people. Allahﷻ sent us a book named the **Qur'an** to guide us.

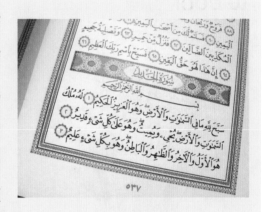

## Allahﷻ provides

Allahﷻ **provides** air, food, and water. To provide means to give or to make something ready for use. He provides air, food, water, sunlight, and everything else we need to live. If there was no air, we could not breathe. If the air was dirty, we would become sick. If there was no water, we would die of thirst. If there was no sunlight, the world would become dark and nothing on earth could live.

Allahﷻ is so kind to give us day and night. The day is for working and the night is for sleeping. If there was no daylight, then the world would be dark and cold. Everything would be **frozen**. If there was no nighttime, then the world would be too hot. The world would be drier than a **desert**.

Allah﷾ provides everything we need to eat. We need fruits, vegetables, and meat to survive. We need rice, corn, cereal, and other types of food. He provides cows, chickens and fish for us to eat.

Allah﷾ makes seeds grow into plants and vegetables. He provides soil, rain, sunshine, and the right temperatures so that seeds can grow. He does all these things because He loves us.

## Allah﷾ protects

Allah﷾ also **protects** us from danger. To protect means to keep someone or something safe from harm or injury. When we have difficulties, only Allah﷾ **rescues** us. When enemies want to harm us, it is Allahﷻ who protects us. When ships sail on a stormy sea, only Allahﷻ protects them. When we ride in cars and on buses, only Allahﷻ saves us from danger.

## Allahﷻ gives honor

Only Allahﷻ has the power to give **honor** to someone. When He gives honor, nobody can take it away. He can make someone a king or a famous person. It is in His power.

## Life and death

Life and death are in Allah'sﷻ hands. Only He can give life. Nobody else can give life. A doctor might treat a patient to help him or her live, but Allahﷻ decides how long the person will live.

## Many other things

Allahﷻ does so many other things so that we can live comfortably on earth. Allahﷻ is so kind to give us different **seasons**. Fruits and vegetables can grow when the seasons change. He gave us rain, so all plants can grow.

If we become sick, Allahﷻ helps us get better. He takes away our pain. Allahﷻ allows us to learn how to speak, read, and write. Allahﷻ made us better than the animals.

**Words that I learned today:**
Blessings • Frozen • Desert • Seasons • Forgives
Al-Aziz • Rescue • Guides • Honor •

1. Circle T if the sentence is true. Circle F if the sentence is false.

There are no defects in Allah's﷽ creations.          (T)  F

Allah﷽ creates and perfects.                          (T)  F

Allah﷽ allows us to learn how to speak and read.     (T)  F

A doctor gives life and death.                        T  (F)

Allah﷽ provides everything for a seed to grow.       (T)  F

2. Fill in the blanks with the right word from the box.

| danger   famous   frozen   guides   honor |

Allah﷽ has the power to give _honor_ to someone.

Allah﷽ can make someone a king or _famous_ .

If there was no sun, everything in the world would
become _frozen_ .

When we ride in cars and on buses, only Allah﷽ protects
us from _danger_ .

Allah﷽ _guides_ us so that we do not make mistakes.

3. Find the following words in the word search puzzle.

AZIZ   PLANTS   CREATE   GUIDE   FORGIVE   OWNER   DEFECT

```
C   K   O   U   A   Z   I   Z
R   I   E   C   V   A   Y   F
E   F   O   R   G   I   V   E
A   T   A   E   R   C   Y   C
T   S   P   L   A   N   T   S
E   O   W   N   E   R   W   Z
W   V   G   U   I   D   E   N
H   D   E   F   E   C   T   V
```

4. In order to guide us, what did Allahﷻ send?

   A.  Air and water

   B.  The Qur'an

   C. Plants and vegetables

5. What is the meaning of the word al-Aziz?

   A.  Protector

   B.  Provider

   C. The Powerful

# Allahﷻ: *What Does He Not Do?*

Assalamu alaikum. Welcome to the class. Let us begin by coloring the sleeping baby

## What Allah ﷻ does not do

In the previous lesson, we learned that Allah ﷻ does many things better than we do. He does these things because He is Powerful and Mighty. Today we will learn many things that Allah ﷻ does not do. When He chooses not to do something, it does not mean He has no power. It means He does not want to do it.

## Allah ﷻ does not sleep

All living beings must sleep. Most animals sleep at night. Some animals sleep during the day and hunt at night. The main reasons for sleep are to **rest** and **regain** energy. Human beings also need to sleep. If we do not sleep for a long time, we become **confused**. After a good night's sleep, we wake up **refreshed**. Sometimes people take a **nap** during the day. Daytime naps help people rest and regain energy.

 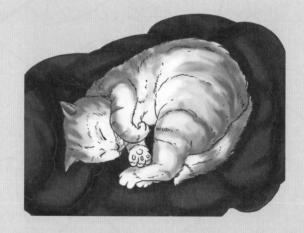

Allah ﷻ is not like us. He does not sleep or take naps. He does not get tired, therefore, He does not need to rest. This indicates Allah ﷻ is always looking out for us.

## Allah does not eat

Human beings eat food to **survive**. We need breakfast, lunch, and dinner. In between these meals, we might eat more. If we do not drink water, we get thirsty. All animals eat and drink. Even plants need food and water to survive.

Allah does not need to eat or drink to survive. He is **ever living**. He lives on His own. Allah is not like us. In surah **Ikhlas**, He says:

$$\text{وَلَمْ يَكُن لَّهُۥ كُفُوًا أَحَدٌ}$$

**Wa lam yakul-llahu kufuan ahad**

It means: **And there is none equal to or like Allah.**

From this we understand that Allah does not need all the things we do to survive. He is not like us.

## Allah never does wrong

Sometimes we do the wrong things. Pushing, hitting, and name calling are wrongs we do to others. Sometimes people cheat others. Sometimes we do wrong to ourselves. Not taking a bath, not wearing clean clothes, and not worshipping Allah are examples of doing wrong to ourselves. Sometimes one country attacks another country for the wrong reasons.

Allah﷾ never tells us to do something that is wrong. Allah﷾ never tells us to worship false gods. Allah﷾ never does things that are unfair. Even if someone does something wrong to us, Allah﷾ will never do wrong to us.

## Allah﷾ never tricks

Sometimes our friends **trick** us. It can be fun to play a simple trick. For example, parents play **peek-a-boo** with their babies. Sometimes we play tricks with simple games. For example:

<table>
<tr>
<td>

Ask someone what color are the two words below:

**GREEN**

**YELLOW**

</td>
<td>

How many animals are in the image?

</td>
</tr>
</table>

Did they say green and yellow? Should they have said red and purple? The colors of the two words are red and purple. In the second box, did you see all five animals? There are many funny mind questions available to trick a friend.

Some people lie to their parents. Sometimes people make a **promise** and break their promise. Sometimes bad people **rob** others. Sometimes people cheat others.

- Allah﷾ never lies.

- Allah﷾ never plays tricks on us.

- Allah﷾ never breaks His promise.

- Allah﷾ never robs people.

## Allah﷾ never turns away

Sometimes, if we are busy doing something, we do not hear our parents call us. Sometimes we pretend not to hear what our friends tell us. When we are asleep, we might not hear loud noises. Sometimes when a friend asks for something, we turn away. If a phone connection is bad, you might not hear your friend talking.

Allah﷾ never turns away from our call. When we **pray** to Allah﷾, He always listens. Allah﷾ never sleeps, so He is always there to hear us. We should always remember to pray to Allah﷾.

## Changing ourselves

Allah﷾ loves us so much that He is always ready to help us. In order for Him to help us, we must first help ourselves. So, how do we help ourselves?

If we are having difficulty, Allah﷾ wants us to try to remove the difficulty. Only then will He help us. If we want to do well on an exam, we must study carefully. Then when we see our grade, we become happy. This is because we tried to help ourselves, and then Allahﷻ helped us.

If a person has money problems, he or she should try to take care of these problems. May be he or she should find a good job and work hard. Only after someone tries their best, will Allahﷻ help.

## Never unfair

In our daily lives, sometimes we are **unfair** to others. If we like someone, sometimes we try to ignore their faults. If we do not like someone, sometimes we try to find fault with them. We might even **bully** others in school. Allahﷻ does not treat people unfairly. He treats everybody equally.

## No injustice

Sometimes we fail to do **justice** to people. If someone makes a small mistake, we might punish the person harshly. Sometimes we ignore big mistakes. Sometimes we cover up a bad action. Our government sometimes fails to deliver justice. The police cannot capture a **culprit**, or a judge does not punish a **guilty** person. Allahﷻ never does **injustice** to anybody. Each and every person is judged fairly and correctly.

## Never gets even

To get even with someone means to take **revenge**. Sometimes we take revenge on a person for a wrong done to us. We want to get even with the person by harming him or her. Allahﷻ does not take revenge. He never tries to get even with people. He is merciful.

## Not miserly

A **miser** is a person who loves to collect money but does not want to spend it. Allahﷻ does not act miserly. He has the **treasure** of the entire world. He gives to everybody in a way that is best for them. He gives some people more money than others, but He always gives. Allahﷻ knows who needs it the most.

**Words that I learned today:**
Refresh • Confused • Nap • Promise • Trick • Ikhlas
Culprit • Guilty • Injustice • Revenge • Miser

1. Which of the following things does Allah ﷻ not do?

   A. Ikhlas

   B. Survive

   C. Sleep

2. Why does Allah ﷻ not do things that we normally do?

   A. Because He is ever Living.

   B. Because He is not like us.

   C. Because He is in Heaven.

3. Which surah says Allah ﷻ is not like us?

   A. Surah Ikhlas.

   B. Surah an-Nas.

   C. Surah al-Falaq.

4. Write the meaning of "Wa lam yakul-llahu kufuan ahad."

   there is none like Allah swt

5. Circle T if the sentence is true. Circle F if the sentence is false.

| | |
|---|---|
| Allahﷻ takes a short nap at midnight. | T **(F)** |
| We need to sleep to regain our energy. | **(T)** F |
| Allahﷻ never tricks us. | **(T)** F |
| A miser collects money but does not spend it. | **(T)** F |
| Sometimes we get even with others by taking revenge. | **(T)** F |
| Allahﷻ never does injustice to others. | **(T)** F |

5. Fill in the blanks using the correct words from the box below.

> survive   nap   pray   turns   sleep   promise

Allahﷻ never breaks His __promise__.

When we __pray__ to Allahﷻ He always listens.

Allahﷻ does not __sleep__ or take a __nap__ to rest.

Allahﷻ does not need things that we do to __survive__.

Allahﷻ never __turns__ away from us.

# The Qur'an

Assalamu alaikum. Welcome to the class. Let us begin by coloring this Qur'an and its stand (rehal).

## Book of Allah ﷻ

The Qur'an is a book from Allah ﷻ. All the words you see in the Qur'an are from Allah ﷻ. He sent these words to our Nabi Muhammad ﷺ. Our Nabi Muhammad ﷺ did not write the book. Allah ﷻ sent the book to **guide** people to live a good life. The Qur'an is in the **Arabic** language.

## How was the book sent?

About 1,400 years ago, during the month of **Ramadan**, Nabi Muhammad ﷺ spent a few nights in a **cave** near Makkah. Alone in the cave, Nabi Muhammad ﷺ thought about how to help his people.

One night during Ramadan, angel **Jibril** (A) went to the cave. He brought **five** sentences from the Qur'an. The sentences in the Qur'an are called **Ayat**, or **signs**. Here is the first ayat:

### Iqra' Bi-smi Rabbika al-Ladhi Khalaqa

It means: Read! In the Name of your Rabb, Who has created.

Allah ﷻ sent the Qur'an through angel Jibril (A). Jibril (A) continued to bring a few ayat or small sections of the Qur'an. It took 23 years to complete the Qur'an.

## Saving the Qur'an

Whenever Nabi Muhammadﷺ received verses from the Qur'an, he first memorized them. Then he asked his **followers** to write them down. The followers saved these pages containing the verses. The followers also memorized the Qur'an. In this way, the Qur'an was saved correctly.

## Organizing the Qur'an

For 23 years, **thousands** of ayat were sent to Nabi Muhammadﷺ. But writing down the Qur'an was not enough. It also had to be **organized**. To organize means to arrange something in a certain manner.

Angel Jibril (A) advised Nabi Muhammadﷺ on how to arrange the Qur'an. Nabi Muhammadﷺ arranged the ayat carefully.

The Qur'an has 114 chapters. A chapter of the Qur'an is called a **surah**. Some surahs are short and some are long. Surah **Fatihah** is the first surah in the Qur'an.

The Qur'an can be divided into 30 parts, or **juz**. This is done to make reading easier. The last juz contains many short surahs. Many of the surahs that we memorize are in the last juz of the Qur'an. Some surahs came to the Nabiﷺ when he was in Makkah. Some surahs came to him when he was in Madinah.

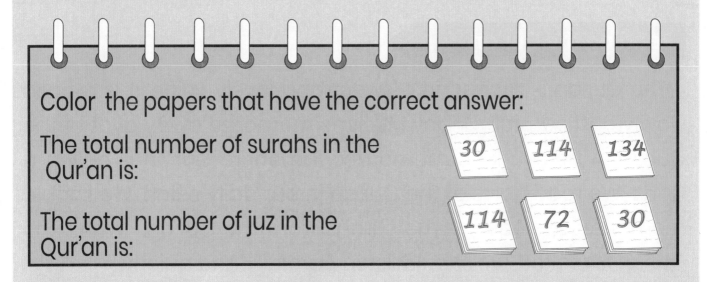

Color the papers that have the correct answer:

The total number of surahs in the Qur'an is:   30   114   134

The total number of juz in the Qur'an is:   114   72   30

### Is the Qur'an correct?

The Qur'an was sent to Nabi Muhammadﷺ about 1,400 years ago. Even though so many years have passed, the Qur'an is still correct. Every word in the Qur'an today is the same as it was then. Not a single word of the Qur'an has changed in the last 1,400 years. Allahﷻ protects it from any changes.

## For whom is the Qur'an?

The Qur'an was first sent to the people in Arabia. The Arabs were the first people to be guided by the Qur'an. Through them, the Qur'an reached many other places. The Qur'an is a book for all people all over the world. It is a guide for everyone. It tells us to follow the **Right Path**.

## Reading the Qur'an

The Qur'an is **recited** in a sweet and lovely voice. It is recited slowly and carefully. Many Muslims memorize every ayat of the Qur'an. A person who memorizes the entire Qur'an is called a **Hafiz**. We read parts of the Qur'an in our daily salah. We should memorize at least some surahs from the Qur'an. When the Qur'an is recited, we should listen carefully and quietly.

## Translation of the Qur'an

Some Muslims do not fully understand Arabic. They try to understand the Qur'an by reading in Arabic and then using a **translation**. Reading a translation means reading a book in another language. The Qur'an has been translated into many languages. The best way to read and understand the Qur'an is to read it in Arabic.

## No new book

Before Nabi Muhammadﷺ Allahﷻ sent books to many other Nabi. Those books were lost or damaged. Therefore, Allahﷻ sent His final and complete **message** in the Qur'an. Allahﷻ will not send any more books. The Qur'an is the final book from Allahﷻ. Nabi Muhammadﷺ is the Last Nabi.

The teachings of the Qur'an are the best teachings.

A _hafiz_ is a person who memorizes the entire Qur'an.

Some surahs came to Nabiﷺ in _Madina_, and some came to him in _makkah_

Will Allahﷻ send any other books after the Qur'an? no no NO

**Words that I learned today:**
Jibril • Verses • Ayat • Ramadan • Surah • Juz
Right Path • Hafiz • Translation • Recite

1. Draw a line from left to right to complete each sentence. The first sentence is done for you.

The teachings of the Qur'an    the Right Path.

It took 23 years    chapters.

The Qur'an has 114    are the best.

The Qur'an shows us    written in Arabic.

The Qur'an is    to complete the Qur'an.

2. Circle T if the sentence is true. Circle F if the sentence is false.

Allah﷾ sent two more books after the Qur'an.    T  F

The Qur'an is only for the Imam to read.    T  F

It took 1,400 years to complete the Qur'an.    T  F

A hafiz is a person who memorized the Qur'an.    T  F

The Qur'an is the best book from Allah﷾.    T  F

The first surah in the Qur'an is Al-e-Imran.    T  F

3. Color the correct oval. A chapter in the Qur'an is called:

Ramadan    Jibril    ~~Surah~~

4. The number of chapters in the Qur'an are:

23    ~~114~~    400

5. The number of juz in the Qur'an is:

23    ~~30~~    93

6. Allah﷾ sent the Qur'an in:

~~Arabic~~    Persian    English

7. Fill in the blanks with the correct word from the box below.

| path    Jibril    last    words |

All the _words_ in the Qur'an are from Allah﷾.

The Qur'an shows us the Right _path_.

Nabi Muhammadﷺ is the _last_ Nabi.

_Jibril_ (A) brought the Qur'an to Nabi Muhammadﷺ.

# Hadith and Sunnah

Assalamu alaikum. Welcome to the class. Let us begin by coloring the six books of hadith.

## Hadith and sunnah

Nabi Muhammadﷺ lived hundreds of years before we were born. Many people listened to him carefully and watched his actions. They told others about what the Nabiﷺ said and did. The sayings of the Nabiﷺ are known as **Hadith**. Many hadith were narrated by Nabi Muhammad'sﷺ family or close followers. They saw or heard many things that Nabi Muhammadﷺ did or said. Therefore, their narrations are included in hadith.

The way Nabiﷺ lived and worked is called the **Sunnah**. When we read hadith, we learn about the sunnah. There are **six** books of hadith. These six books have thousands of hadith.

## Why hadith and sunnah?

In the Qur'an, Allahﷻ says that the life and activities of Nabi Muhammadﷺ are a beautiful example. The two questions are: What are these examples? Where can we find them?

The Qur'an mentions several important examples of our Nabi'sﷺ activities. Some of these examples are brief. Many others are not mentioned. In order to learn the details, we read the books of hadith. These hadith tell us the things that Nabi Muhammadﷺ allowed us to do and the things that he told us to avoid. The books of hadith are important for Muslims.

The sayings of the Nabi ﷺ are called: _hadith_

The actions of the Nabi ﷺ are called: _sunnah_

How many books of hadith are available? _six_

## How were hadith made?

When Nabi Muhammad ﷺ was alive, many people memorized his teachings. They also passed on these teachings to their children and grandchildren.

As time passed, many people in Arabia became Muslim. Many lived far away from Makkah and Madinah—the two places our Nabi ﷺ lived. Many of these people had never seen the Nabi ﷺ. They wanted to know what Nabi Muhammad ﷺ said and what he did. They learned about the Nabi's ﷺ life through people who had spent time with him.

One day, Nabi Muhammad ﷺ passed away. Over time, many of the people who had spent time with the Nabi ﷺ also passed away. People thought they would begin to forget what the Nabi ﷺ did and said. So they began to write down what they remembered. Several wise people began to write down hadith.

## Imam Bukhari

A wise person named **Imam al-Bukhari** collected the **ahadith** that people remembered. More than one hadith is called ahadith. Imam al-Bukhari spent his entire life collecting ahadith. He traveled to distant places and met people who knew a hadith. Some people told him false ahadith that Nabi Muhammadﷺ never said. Imam al-Bukhari was wise and found out which ahadith were correct and which ones were false. He collected only the correct ahadith. His collections are known as correct, or **Sahih**. His book is called **Sahih Bukhari**.

## Other collectors

After Imam al-Bukhari, five other Imams also collected hadith. With their five books and Sahih Bukhari, we have a total of six books of hadith. These six books are known as **Sahih Sitta**, or the **True Six**. Look at page 54. Can you name some of the collectors of hadith?

## The Qur'an and hadith

The Qur'an is the most important book in Islam. The books of hadith books are the second-most important books. Hadith give us details about many Islamic laws. The Qur'an tells us to give zakat and to donate to charity. How much should we give in zakat? Hadith give us the details.

The books of hadith have many good **teachings** about how to lead our lives. Our dear Nabi Muhammadﷺ is not with us, but we can learn about him from the books of hadith.

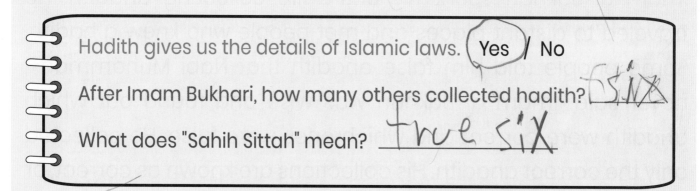

Hadith gives us the details of Islamic laws. ( Yes )/ No

After Imam Bukhari, how many others collected hadith? S̶i̶x̶

What does "Sahih Sittah" mean? True six

**Words that I learned today:**
Hadith • Sunnah • Imam al-Bukhari • Ahadith
Sahih • Sahih Sitta • Teachings

1. Draw a line from left to right to match each word to its correct meaning.

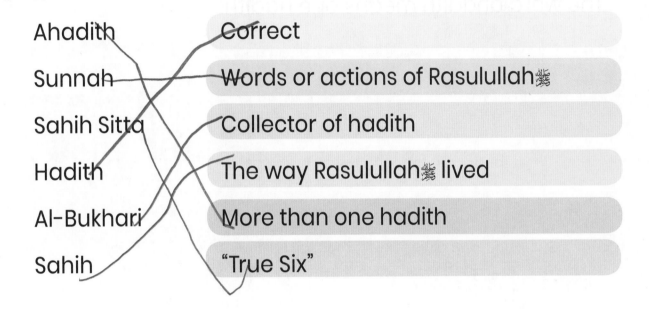

Ahadith      Correct

Sunnah      Words or actions of Rasulullahﷺ

Sahih Sitta      Collector of hadith

Hadith      The way Rasulullahﷺ lived

Al-Bukhari      More than one hadith

Sahih      "True Six"

2. Why did people write down the words and actions of the Rasulﷺ? Circle all the correct choices.

A. People wanted to know how the Rasulﷺ lived and worked.

B. People thought hadith would be forgotten unless they wrote them down.

C. People wanted to pass time by writing books.

D. People wanted to slowly forget the Nabiﷺ.

3. Circle T if the sentence is true. Circle F if the sentence is false.

The six books of hadith are called the "Sahih Saba." T F

Imam al-Bukhari collected many ahadith. T F

The word ahadith means one hadith. T F

# Unit 2: Our Ibadat

This unit presents an overview of the Five Pillars of Islam. Although we covered the basics of the Five Pillars in Level 1, a renewed discussion with some additional details is worthwhile. Our Ibadat is based on the Five Pillars of Islam. These pillars are the framework for our worship and a demonstration of our commitment to our faith. No matter how sincerely a person may believe in Islam, our religion requires that faith be put into action and practice. An early understanding of the Five Pillars will help children progress through other areas of curriculum in future years.

# Unit 2: Our Ibadat

## Shahadah: *The First Pillar*

This lesson covers the basics of the first pillar of Islam. Shahadah is the fundamental idea of Islam; without it, one cannot be a Muslim. The core concept of each of the five-pillars is introduced, one pillar at a time.

## Salat: *The Second Pillar*

After declaring Shahadah, the next step is to demonstrate faith in action by performing salat. Therefore, salat is the second pillar of Islam. Performing salat is a daily duty for all Muslims. This lesson covers the basics of the second pillar. Emphasis is placed on the practice of regular salat.

## Zakat: *The Third Pillar*

Zakat is an important duty upon all qualified individuals who have surplus earning. In this context, students will learn that salat is a personal duty. Zakat is a duty to the community. Thus, Islam is not only about improving the self, it is also about the people around us. This lesson focuses on the third pillar of Islam. Students are encouraged at an early age to learn the value of giving and sharing.

## Fasting: *The Fourth Pillar*

This lesson introduces students to an annual duty of Islam—fasting during Ramadan. Fasting is the fourth pillar of Islam. Fasting creates greater awareness of God. Fasting brings us closer to Allah. In this lesson, students will learn the rules and exception for fasting.

## Hajj: *The Fifth Pillar*

Hajj is a once-in-a-lifetime duty. This lesson explains the basic concept of the fifth pillar of Islam. In this chapter, students will learn the most important steps of performing Hajj. They will also learn about some of the important places where pilgrims visit during Hajj.

## Wudu: *Cleaning Before Salat*

Before we can do salat, we have to make wudu. The steps of wudu are important. In this lesson, students will learn these steps.

# Shahadah: *The First Pillar*

Assalamu alaikum. Welcome to the class. Let us color the words below.

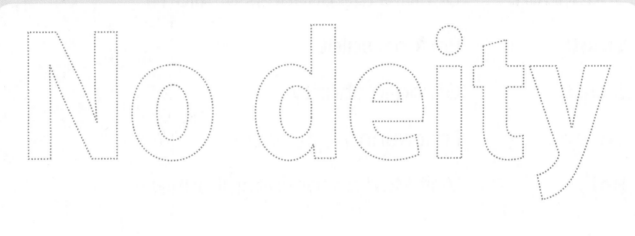

No deity but Allah

## Islam has five pillars

The religion of Islam is similar to a house. It has five pillars. These pillars make the Islam strong. These pillars tell us what we should do to be good Muslims. These pillars are the five basic duties of all Muslims. These five duties are:

**Shahadah:** Declare the oneness of Allah ﷻ

**Salat:** Perform salat

**Zakat:** Giving in charity

**Sawm:** Fast during Ramadan

**Hajj:** Visit Makkah for special duties

## The first pillar

Shahadah is the first pillar of Islam. Shahadah is stating our most important belief. Our most important belief is Allah ﷻ is the only God. We are Muslim because we believe and declare that Allah ﷻ is the only God.

When we say the Shahadah, we declare that Allah ﷻ is the only God, and Muhammad ﷺ is His Rasul. In Arabic, we say:

أَشْهَدُ أَنْ لَا إِلَهَ إِلَّا اللَّهُ

**Ash-hadu an la ilaha illal-lahu**

وَأَشْهَدُ أَنَّ مُحَمَّدًا رَسُولُ اللَّهِ

**wa ash-hadu anna Muhammadur Rasulullah**

## We worship Allah

We pray only to Allah. He is our Master and He created us. We always need Allah. We **worship** only Allah.

We do not worship anyone else. Allah is the one who created us. Nobody else can help us the way Allah helps us. Allah is the only **deity**. A deity is the god we worship.

Allah sent many nabis and rasuls. The nabis and rasuls taught people the only religion of Islam. Nabi Muhammad taught us the complete Islam. He showed us how to live our lives. Allah sent us the Qur'an through Nabi Muhammad. Our Nabi passed away, but the Qur'an remains with us. When we believe in Nabi Muhammad, we believe in the Qur'an, which was revealed to him.

## Two parts of Shahadah

Shahadah has two parts. Both parts are necessary for it to be complete. The first part reminds us that Allah is the only God. The second part says that Muhammad is the Rasul of Allah. Let us look closely at the two parts of Shahadah.

## The first part

**La ilaha illal-lahu:** This is the first part of the Shahadah. This part declares two things:

**La ilaha:** There is no god.

**Illal-lahu:** Except Allahﷻ.

First, we say there is no god. This means no other gods can exist. Therefore, the sun, the moon, idols, cows, owls, elephants and other objects are not gods. Some people say they are gods. This is not true.

Second, we declare that Allahﷻ is the only God. The first part of Shahadah states there is no deity but Allahﷻ. This means that we can only worship Allahﷻ.

## The second part

**Muhammadur Rasulullah:** This is the second part of the Shahadah. This part declares that Muhammadﷺ is the **Rasul** of Allahﷻ. We follow the teachings of Muhammadﷺ. However, we do not worship Muhammadﷺ. We worship only Allahﷻ.

The Shahadah is these two parts together: "**Ash-hadu an la ilaha illal-lahu**" and "**wa ash-hadu anna Muhammadur Rasulullah.**"

## We give witness

Shahadah means to give **witness**. We can give witness when we know something clearly. Muslims clearly know there is no deity but Allah. As Muslims, we must say the Shahadah and believe in it. When a non-Muslim person wants to become a Muslim, he or she says the Shahadah.

Nabi Muhammad was a rasul. A rasul is a person who brings messages from Allah. Nabi Muhammad brought us the Qur'an. As Muslim, we believe in all the messages in the Qur'an.

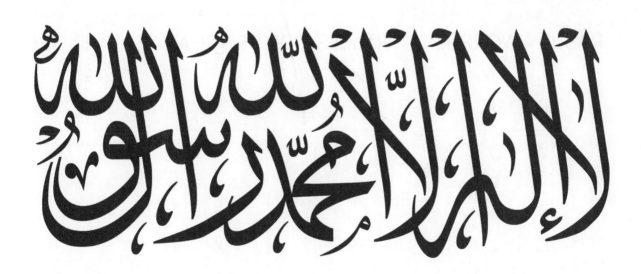

**Words that I learned today:**

Worship • Deity • Rasul • Witness
La ilaha illal-lahu Muhammadur Rasulullah

1. Write Yes if the sentence is correct. Write No if the sentence is wrong.

We worship only Allahﷻ. _Yes_

We may worship two gods. _No_

We do not worship Nabi Muhammadﷺ. _Yes_

2. Find the following words in the puzzle.

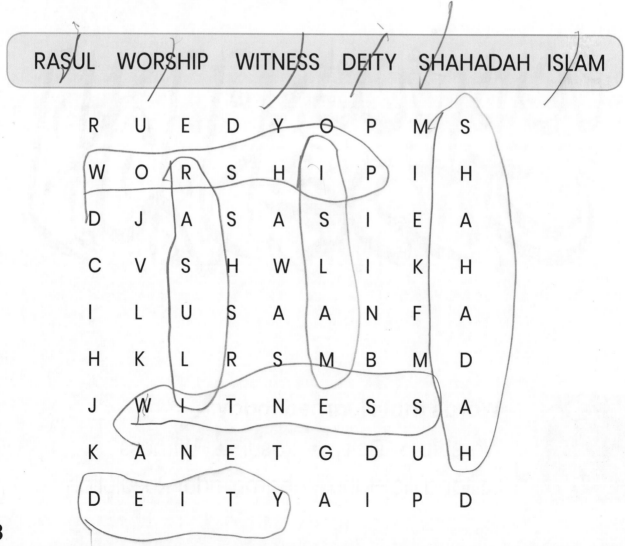

RASUL    WORSHIP    WITNESS    DEITY    SHAHADAH    ISLAM

```
R  U  E  D  Y  O  P  M  S
W  O  R  S  H  I  P  I  H
D  J  A  S  A  S  I  E  A
C  V  S  H  W  L  I  K  H
I  L  U  S  A  A  N  F  A
H  K  L  R  S  M  B  M  D
J  W  I  T  N  E  S  S  A
K  A  N  E  T  G  D  U  H
D  E  I  T  Y  A  I  P  D
```

3. Circle T if the sentence is true. Circle F if the sentence is false.

| | | |
|---|---|---|
| We worship both Allah ﷻ and Nabi Muhammad ﷺ. | T | **F** |
| Shahadah means to give witness. | **T** | F |
| Allah ﷻ is the only deity. | **T** | F |
| Nabi Muhammad ﷺ was a rasul of Allah ﷻ. | **T** | F |
| Nabi Muhammad ﷺ taught the complete Islam. | **T** | F |
| We can be Muslim without believing in Shahadah. | T | **F** |

4. Memorize the Shahadah. Be ready to recite it in front of the class next week!

# Salat: *The Second Pillar*

Assalamu alaikum. Welcome to the class. Let us color the area of a masjid where an Imam stands to lead the salat.

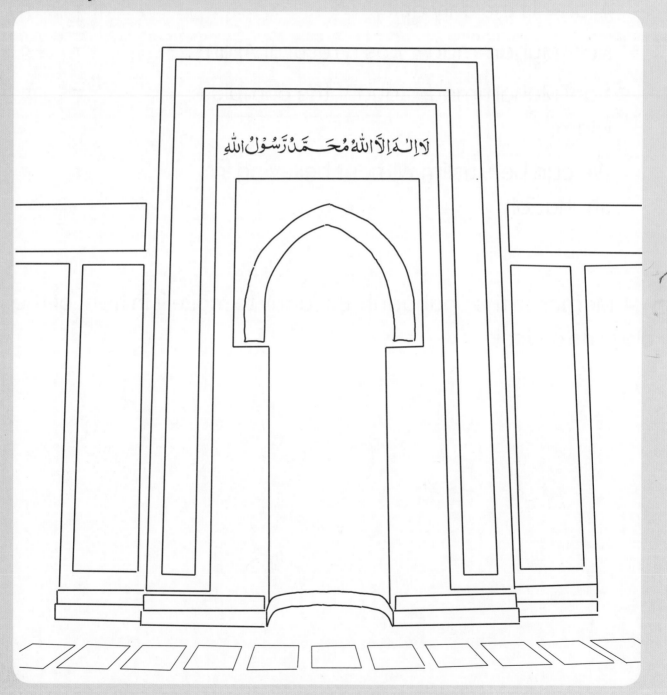

## The second pillar

**Salat** is the second pillar of Islam. Salat, or prayer, is done **five** times every day. These prayers are made at specific times. All Muslims, young or old, men or women, must do salat. It is a duty for us. The five salat every day remind us of Allah ﷻ and all His blessings to us.

The names and times of the five salat are:

1. **Fajr**: early morning, after dawn and before sunrise

2. **Dhuhr**: just after noon

3. **Asr**: late afternoon

4. **Maghrib**: right after sunset

5. **'Isha**: night, after Maghrib salah

| Fajr | Dhuhr | Asr | Maghrib | 'Isha |

## Basic steps of salat

Salat has many steps. We follow these steps carefully. When we make salat, we stand facing the direction of the **Ka'bah** in

Makkah. This direction is called **Qiblah**. During salat, we follow certain rules. Our Rasulullahﷺ taught us these steps and rules.

## Alone or in a group

Salat can be done alone or in a group. It is always better to pray in a group. When we are in a group, an **Imam** leads the salat. The Imam is the leader of the salat. The Imam stands in front, and everyone else stands behind him. When we pray in a group, we stand in **rows**. All the boys and men stand in front. All the girls and women stand behind the boys and men.

We can do the five daily salat alone or with a group of people. Some salat must be done with other people. On Fridays, we do salat in a group. This is called Salatul **Jumuah**. When we pray Salatul Jumuah, we do not pray Salatul Dhuhr. On the days of Eid, we do salat in a group. Many people attend the Eid salat.

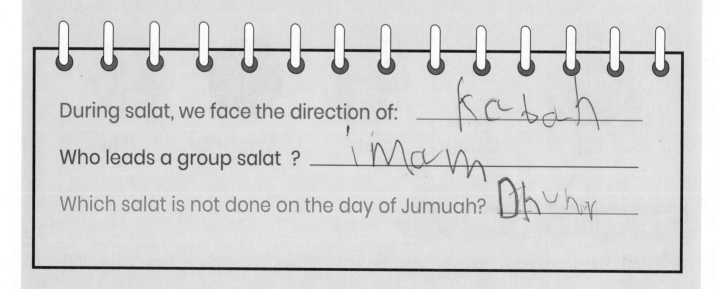

During salat, we face the direction of: _Kabah_

Who leads a group salat ? _Imam_

Which salat is not done on the day of Jumuah? _Dhuhr_

## Why not all together?

Do you know why the times of salat are spread out over the day? Why can we not make all our salat together? Allah taught us to do salat at different times of day. Muslims should remember Allah all day, even with our schools, jobs, and activities. Dhuhr prayer is in the middle of our school and work day. During school and work hours, we should not forget Allah. Similarly, during other busy times, we should not forget Allah.

Doing salat brings us closer to Allah. We should do each salah at its correct time. Doing each salah on time shows that we follow Islam and that we have faith in Allah.

## Before salah

Before salah, we should make **wudu**. Wudu means we wash our face, hands, and wipe our head and feet. Sometimes we might have to take a shower. We should not pray with dirty clothes. The place where we do salat must also be clean.

Before salah, a call for prayer is made. This call is the **Adhan**. This call is made in a nice, **melodious** voice. The adhan is a reminder that it is time for salah. Do you know the words of the adhan? The words are easy to remember, so you can learn them quickly. Then you can be a **muadhdhin** in your home, which means that you make the call for prayer!

Whenever you hear a muadhdhin calling you to salah, leave your activity, and join the salah. Allah ﷻ **accepts** the salah and rewards us for praying.

## Types of salat

There are different types of salat, but all salat have some common steps. The five daily salat are the **compulsory** ones. This means they must be performed. There are also **sunnah** salat, and extra salat. The extra salat are called **nawafil** salat. It is good for us to perform these extra salah. These extra salah are done before or after the five daily salah.

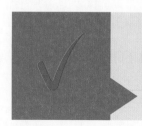

**Words that I learned today:**

Ka'bah • Qiblah • Imam • Rows • Jumuah • Wudu
Adhan • Melodious • Muadhdhin • Compulsory • Nawafil

# Steps of Salah

Stand for salāt facing the direction of the Ka'bah.

(Front and side view)

Raise hands for takbir. Place them on the belly to recite sūrahs.

Bend down for ruku.

(Front and side view)

Stand up from ruku.

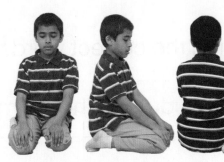

Bow down to make sujud.

Sit down from sujud, jalsa position.

(Front, side, and back view)

Second sujud from jalsa position.

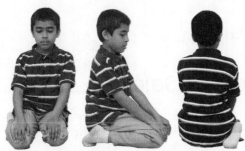

After the 2nd raka'at, sit down after 2nd sujud to recite tashahud.

Complete salāt—turn face, first to the right and then to the left for salam.

1. Write the names of the five prayers in the order they are done in a day.

| 1 |  Fajr | 2 | 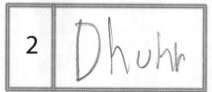 Dhuhr | 3 |  Asr |
|---|---|---|---|---|---|

| 4 |  Maghrib | 5 | Isha |
|---|---|---|---|

2. Fill in the blanks using the correct words from the box below.

> faith   Jumuah   Wudu   Adhan   Imam   Qiblah

We clean ourselves before Salah by doing __Wudu__.

The direction we face while we pray is the __Qiblah__.

The __Imah__ leads the salah.

The group prayer on Fridays is called Salatul __Jumah__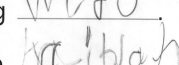

The call to prayer is known as the __Adhan__.

We make salah because we have __faith__ in Allah ﷻ.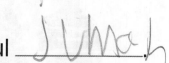

3. Draw a line from left to right to match five salah to their correct times.

Fajr

Dhuhr

Asr

Maghrib

'Isha

right after sunset

mid-afternoon

after dawn and before sunrise

at night

just after noon

4. Find the following words in the puzzle.

SALAH   JUMUAH   ADHAN   IMAM   QIBLAH   ACCEPT   PRAY   KABAH

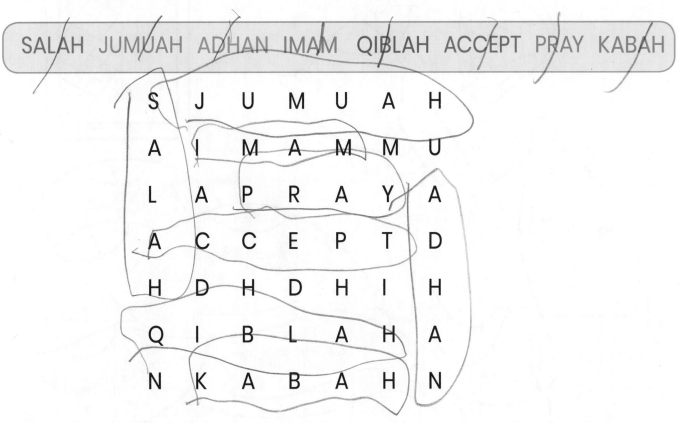

```
S  J  U  M  U  A  H
A  I  M  A  M  M  U
L  A  P  R  A  Y  A
A  C  C  E  P  T  D
H  D  H  D  H  I  H
Q  I  B  L  A  H  A
N  K  A  B  A  H  N
```

5. In the puzzle above, you have not circled some of the letters. With these letters, write the title of the person who calls the adhan. _mudahan_

# Zakat: *The Third Pillar*

Assalamu alaikum. Welcome to the class. Let us begin by coloring Khalid, who is helping a charity.

## Helping the poor

Allah﷾ gave us **wealth**. Our wealth helps us survive. It allows us to buy clothes, food, or homes. Allah﷾ did not give everybody an equal amount of wealth. Some people have more wealth than others. Needy people do not have enough money to buy food or clothes. Allah﷾ tells us that poor people should get a share of our wealth.

The third pillar of Islam is about sharing our wealth with needy people.

## The third pillar

**Zakat** is the third pillar of Islam. The word zakat means to clean or to purify. People pay zakat to purify their wealth. The simple meaning of zakah is **charity**. Charity means donating something to help a needy person. We could give money, food, or clothes to someone who does not have enough. We should help people who are needy.

Salat and fasting are two important duties for all Muslims. The rich and the poor must do salat and fast. Zakat is also an important duty, but only for Muslims who have enough money. People calculate their wealth and savings for the year. Then they donate part of their wealth to the poor.

## Zakat helps the needy

Needy people can do many things with the help of zakat. They can buy food, clothing, and medicine. Zakat helps needy people handle their problems.

People who are rich now may not always be rich. Sometimes people lose their money or their homes. Sometimes a fire or flood might **destroy** a house or business. A person might lose his or her job. When people face problem, zakat can help them. If we give to charity, then people can re-build their homes, start a new business, or buy the things they need to survive.

Sometimes it does not rain for months. Farmers cannot grow **crops** without water. Without crops to sell, farmers become poor. If we help them, they can get new seeds for the next growing season.

## Zakat helps society

Zakat helps to build a good **society**. A society is a large group of people who live and work together. Not everyone in a society is rich. Some people are poor. The rich have a duty to help the poor. Giving zakat reminds us that we live among other people. A good Muslim does not want anyone else to suffer. A rich person cannot give zakat to another rich person. Poor people do not have to give zakat because they do not have enough money.

## Bilal gives Zakat

After learning about zakat, Bilal decided to give zakat from his own money. Bilal is 7 years old. Last month, on his birthday, he received gifts from his friends and family. He received a total of $100. To encourage Bilal, his father told him he could pay $2.50 from this money as zakat. Bilal donated this amount to charity. Zakat is paid on the excess money a person keeps for the year.

## When to give zakat?

Zakat money is given once every year. It is given when a person's wealth is over a certain limit. Zakat can be given any time of year. Most people give zakat during Ramadan.

## The Qur'an on zakat

We should help our needy relatives, neighbors, and even people we do not know. Not only poor people receive money. **Travelers** who have difficulty can receive zakat. The Qur'an tells us who may get zakat and who may not. There are **eight** types of people who can receive zakat.

## Do not waste

We can easily give money to others if we do not **waste** it. We should never waste money. If we do not spend all our money, then we will have enough for ourselves, and we can give some of our saved money to the needy.

**Words that I learned today:**
Zakat • Charity • Destroy • Crops • Society
Travelers • Waste

1. How can zakat help the needy?

_money_

_food_

_med_

2. Name four ways people can help the needy.

A. _give money_

B. _charity_

C. _zakat_

D. _food_

3. Fill in the blanks using the correct words from the box below.

> third    charity    society    waste

_charity_ is giving something to help another person.

Zakat is the _third_ pillar of Islam.

If we _waste_ our money, we cannot help others.

Zakat helps people build a good _society_

**4. Circle T if the sentence is true. Circle F if the sentence is false.**

A man who owns an expensive car should get zakat.    T (F)

A man who has no job and has a hungry family should (T) F
get zakat.

An orphan who needs food and books should get (T) F
zakat.

A family that loses their home in an earthquake should T (F)
get zakat.

A woman who lives in a mansion should get zakat.    T (F)

A man who lost his store in a flood should get zakat.    (T) F

# Sawm: *The Fourth Pillar*

Assalamu alaikum. Welcome to the class. This is Imran's Iftar, after his first day of fasting. Let us color the drawing to make it look yummy.

## Fourth pillar

Islam has five pillars. The fourth pillar of Islam is **Sawm**. The simple meaning of sawm is fasting. Fasting means to avoid eating or drinking. When Muslims fast, they do not eat or drink from **dawn** until sunset.

## The month of fasting

Fasting occurs during the month of **Ramadan**. This is the ninth month of the Islamic calendar. The Islamic calendar begins when we see a new moon. The month of Ramadan also begins when we see a new moon. The month ends when we see another new moon.

## How to begin and end?

Fasting begins at dawn, so we may eat before dawn. Your parents might get up early in the morning—well before breakfast time—to eat some food. This meal is called **suhoor**. They will not eat anything throughout the day. If you have fasted before, you know that you cannot even drink water during the daytime.

When the sun sets, it is time to break the fast. At that time, you eat and drink good food. Your breakfast is at sunset! This meal is called **Iftar**.

Sawm is the ___fourth___ pillar of Islam.

Ramadan is the ___nineth___ month of the Islamic calendar.

We break our fast with a meal called ___Iftar___

### Closeness to Allah ﷻ

Fasting helps us become aware of Allah ﷻ. This allows us to feel closer to Allah ﷻ and become better people. During Ramadan, Muslims pray more and read more chapters of the Qur'an. At home or at the masjid, we pray a special salah at night. This salah is called **Tarawih**.

Fasting is for our benefit. Allah ﷻ rewards those who fast during the month of Ramadan. As you grow older, you should try to fast for more days. In a few years, you will be able to fast during the entire month of Ramadan!

Fasting might seem difficult, but it is not. Allah ﷻ wants to make it easy for us. For this reason, Allah ﷻ says those who are sick and those who are traveling do not need to fast. They can fast on other days. Those who cannot fast due to old age or sickness, can feed the poor instead.

## Three forms of reward

Ramadan brings us three forms of reward. These rewards are spread out over the entire month. Ramadan is the month to receive more blessings, mercy, and forgiveness from Allah﷾. To receive these blessings, we should fast, pray, and remember Allah﷾ many times a day. We should also stay away from all bad actions.

| First 10 days | **Mercy** |
| Second 10 days | **Forgiveness** |
| Last 10 days | **Protection from Fire** |

## The Qur'an in Ramadan

Ramadan is the month Nabi Muhammadﷺ started to receive the Qur'an. One night during Ramadan, Nabi Muhammadﷺ was in a cave in Mount Hira. That night, angel Jibril (A) brought the first five verses of the Qur'an to Nabi Muhammadﷺ.

## Eid al-Fitr

Ramadan is a blessed month. When Ramadan ends, the happy day of **Eid al-Fitr** arrives. We should not fast on this day.

We should thank Allah﷾ for the month of Ramadan. We should enjoy the day of Eid with our families and friends. We should also share our food or money with people who do not have enough.

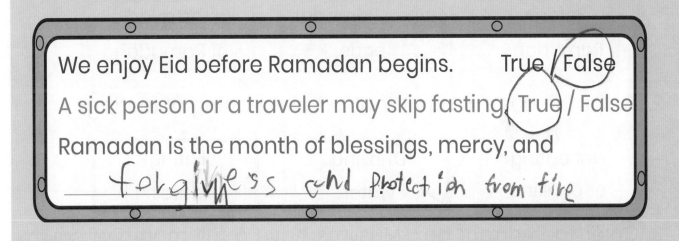

We enjoy Eid before Ramadan begins.     True / False

A sick person or a traveler may skip fasting. True / False

Ramadan is the month of blessings, mercy, and

_forgiveness and protection from fire_

# Eid Mubarak

**Words that I learned today:**

Sawm • Dawn • Ramadan • Iftar • Suhoor
Eid al-Fitr • Tarawih

1. Color the correct box. When is Eid al-Fitr?

| Before Ramadan | When Ramadan ends  | In the middle of Ramadan |

2. Color the correct box. What is the meaning of fasting?

| Not eating or drinking | Drinking water | Eating dates |

3. Color the correct box. Muslims have a full month of sawm during the month of:

| Muharram | Ramadan | Rajab |

4. What is the name of the meal you eat when you break the fast?

Iftar

5. Color this banner for Eid.

6. Draw a line from left to right to match each word to its correct meaning.

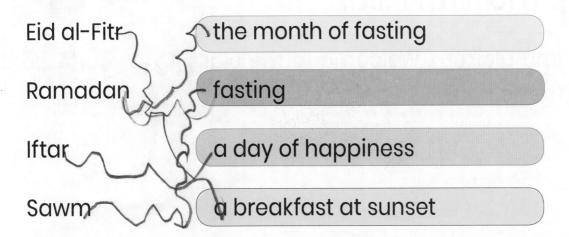

Eid al-Fitr — a day of happiness

Ramadan — the month of fasting

Iftar — a breakfast at sunset

Sawm — fasting

7. Circle the things we do on Eid al-Fitr. Cross out the things we do not do.

Fast

Celebrate

Have fun with family and friends

Share food and money with the poor

# Hajj: *The Fifth Pillar*

Assalamu alaikum. Welcome to the class. Can you trace the path to the Ka'bah?

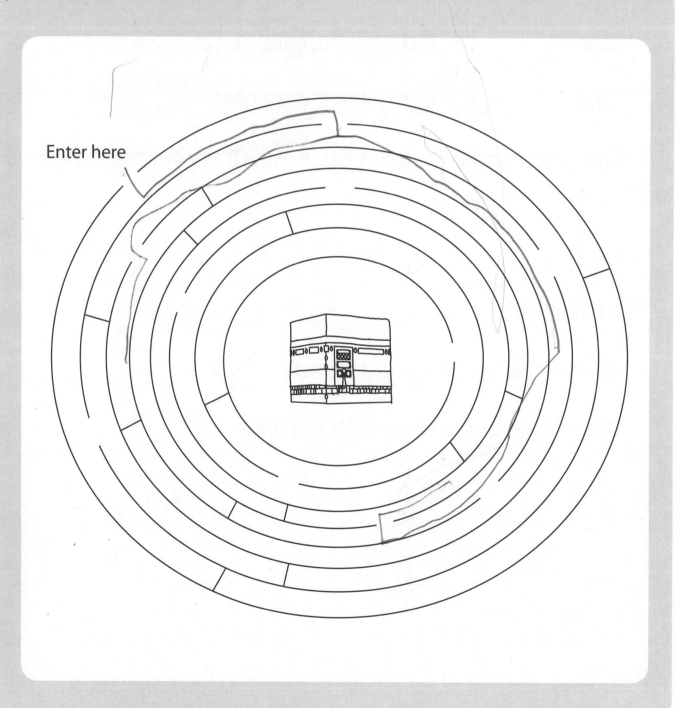

Enter here

## Fifth pillar of Islam

Islam has five pillars. Hajj is the fifth pillar of Islam. Hajj is a **pilgrimage**. Pilgrimage means a journey to a holy place. People who go on a pilgrimage are **pilgrims**. To complete the Hajj, Muslims go to Makkah. They stay there for few days and complete some duties.

## Dhul-Hajj

Hajj occurs once every year. It occurs in the month of **Dhul-Hajj**. Dhul Hajj is the 12th and final month of the Islamic calendar. Muslims from all over the world go to Makkah for Hajj. They arrive by airplanes, ships, buses, and cars.

## A duty for all Muslims

Allahﷻ gave us many duties. Salat is a daily duty. Zakat is a yearly or annual duty. Fasting is an annual duty. Hajj is a once-in-a-lifetime duty. All adult Muslims who are in good health and have ability should go to Hajj at least once in their lifetimes.

## Ibrahim (A) started Hajj

Today Makkah is a large city. Thousands of years ago, it was not even a village. There were no trees or gardens. It was a rocky place, and it was very difficult to find water to drink. Nobody lived in Makkah at that time.  Then Nabi **Ibrahim** (A) brought his family to live in Makkah.

Ibrahim (A) brought his wife, **Hajar**, and his baby son, **Ismail** (A), to Makkah. Baby Ismail (A) became very thirsty, and Hajar searched for water everywhere. She ran several times between two small hills, **Safa** and **Marwah**, looking for water. She and her baby became even more tired and thirsty. Then Allahﷻ gave them a small spring of fresh water gushing out of the rocks. This spring is called **Zamzam**.

When Ismail (A) grew up, he and his father, Ibrahim (A), built the **Ka'bah**. Then they called people to come for Hajj. People began to come to Makkah on camels and on foot, from places near and far.

Mother Hajar had a son named _Ismail_.

The spring in Makkah is known as _ZcmZcm_.

Two small hills in Makkah are Safa and _marwah_.

## Ihram

During Hajj, men wear two pieces of white cloth called **Ihram**. Each Ihram cloth is a simple, plain sheet. This cloth has no stitches on it. One piece is worn around the waist. The other piece is worn over the upper body. All men look alike in their simple, similar clothes. Hajj cannot be done without Ihram. Women do not need to wear white Ihram cloth. Their regular clothing is fine for Hajj.

## Duties of Hajj

Hajj involves several duties. After men put on the **Ihram**, all men and women walk in circles around the Ka'bah. They do this seven times. This walking is called **Tawaf**.

Previously, we learned that Ibrahim (A) and his son, Ismail (A), built the Ka'bah. The

Ka'bah is a brick building. It looks black because a black covering is placed over it. During our salat, we face the direction of the Ka'bah.

A short distance from the Ka'bah are two small hills known as **Safa** and **Marwah**. After the pilgrims walk in circles around the Ka'bah, they walk between these two small hills to remember mother Hajar. They walk seven times between these two hills.

Then everyone goes to a place called Mina. This place has thousands of **tents**. People stay in tents in Mina.

Next the pilgrims go to a place called Arafat. They stay in Arafat for half a day. Here, people pray to Allah﷾ for forgiveness.

On their way back to Mina, the pilgrims spend the night at Muzdalifah. There are no tents to sleep in here. They spend the night under the sky on the ground.

The next morning, the pilgrims return to Mina. There are three large walls in Mina. People throw small stones at these walls. This stone-throwing reminds them to chase Shaitan out of their lives. Then the pilgrims **sacrifice** an animal. Even if we do not go to Hajj, we still sacrifice an animal on that day. This day the day of **Eid al-Adha**. People sacrifice an animal on this day.

There are a few other steps to complete during Hajj. Within a day or two, all the duties of Hajj are completed.

## Remembering Ibrahim (A)

Allah taught us the rules of Hajj. Our Nabi Muhammad showed us how to follow the rules. During Hajj, most of the duties remind us of Ibrahim (A). He was the first to call people to come for Hajj. Going to Hajj teaches us to respond to Allah. We learn to sacrifice for the sake of Allah. Hajj also teaches us to be kind, patient, and **humble**. We are reminded to avoid Shaitan. We learn that Allah helps good people when they have difficulty.

**Words that I learned today:**

Pilgrimage • Pilgrims • Dhul-Hajj • Ibrahim (A)

Hajar • Ismail (A) • Safa • Marwah • Zamzam

Ihram • Tawaf • Mina • Arafat • Sacrifice

1. What happened when baby Ismail (A) was thirsty in Makkah?

_A's mom ran in between two small hills then Allah made a angel make water for ismail (A) and his mom water_

2. Find the following words in the word search puzzle.

PILGRIM    IHRAM    TAWAF    MINA

ARAFAT    ZAMZAM    SAFA

```
J  Z  B  R  M  I  N  A  A
T  A  R  A  F  A  T  X  F
A  M  C  K  O  Y  P  P  I
W  Z  I  R  F  K  I  H  Q
A  A  L  O  G  W  L  A  T
F  M  A  R  H  B  G  J  D
D  B  S  A  F  A  R  J  S
C  Z  N  D  L  H  I  M  C
L  C  I  H  R  A  M  X  T
```

3. Draw a line from left to right to connect the phrases to make a sentence.

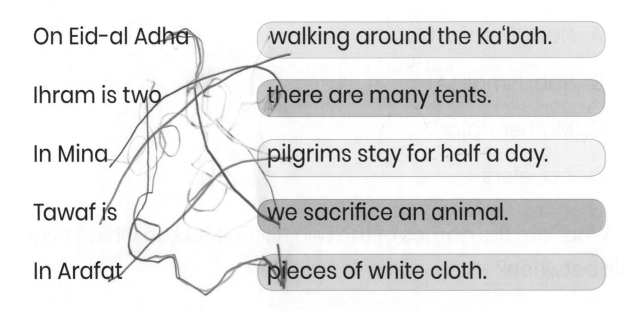

| | |
|---|---|
| On Eid-al Adha | walking around the Ka'bah. |
| Ihram is two | there are many tents. |
| In Mina | pilgrims stay for half a day. |
| Tawaf is | we sacrifice an animal. |
| In Arafat | pieces of white cloth. |

4. Write YES if the sentence is correct. Write NO if it is not correct.

| | |
|---|---|
| All the men wear two pieces of white cloth called Tawaf. | √ |
| Pilgrims throw small stones at large walls in Mina. | √ |
| We should sacrifice an animal on the day of Eid al-Fitr. | √ |
| Hajar found fresh water from a spring named Zamzam. | √ |

5. Ask your parents to help you find surah number 22 in the Qur'an. Then write the name of the surah.

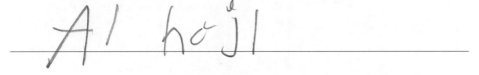

Al hajl

6. Who ran several times between two hills in search of water and then found Zamzam?

    A. Nabi Ibrahim (A).

    B. Nabi Ismail (A).

    C. Mother Hajar.

    D. Travelers.

7. What are the names of the two hills in Makkah which pilgrims walk between?

    A. Marwah and Hira.

    B. Hira and Thawr.

    C. Safa and Sinai.

    D. Safa and Marwah.

8. During Hajj, where do pilgrims go after doing Tawaf?

    A. They go to sacrifice an animal.

    B. They go to celebrate Eid al-Adha.

    C. They go to Mina.

    D. They go to throw stones.

# Wudu: *Cleaning Before Salat*

Assalamu alaikum. Welcome to the class. Can you color this boy who is making wudu?

## Preparing for salat

Before we can do salat, we have to make **wudu**. Making wudu means we prepare our bodies and minds for salat. Wudu is about washing certain parts of our bodies. Allah﷾ will not accept our salat if we do not make wudu. There are certain conditions when our wudu may "break." If our wudu breaks, we have to make wudu again before doing salat.

## Steps of wudu

Allah﷾ says that when we stand up for salat, we should do wudu. Then He describes the steps of wudu. We learn these steps from the Qur'an and from the teachings of Rasulullahﷺ.

We begin with the name of Allah﷾ by saying Bismillahi-r Rahmani-r Rahim. Make an intention to make wudu silently.

| | | |
|---|---|---|
| | 1 | First, we wash our right hand three times. Then we wash our left hand three times. During this step, we wash each hand up to the wrist. |
| | 2 | Next we clean the inside of our mouth. We do this three times. |

| | | |
|---|---|---|
| | **3** | Next we **sniff** water inside our nose. We do this three times. If we need to blow our nose to clear it, this is the time to do it. |
| | **4** | Next we wash our face. We take water in both hands and wash our face from hairline to chin, and from ear to ear. We do this three times. |
| | **5** | Next we wash our right arm three times up to the elbow.  Then we wash our left arm three times up to the elbow. |
| | **6** | Next we wipe our heads with our wet **palms**. We run our palms and fingers down our head. |
| | **7** | Next we clean our ear holes with a finger, and clean the back side of our ears. |

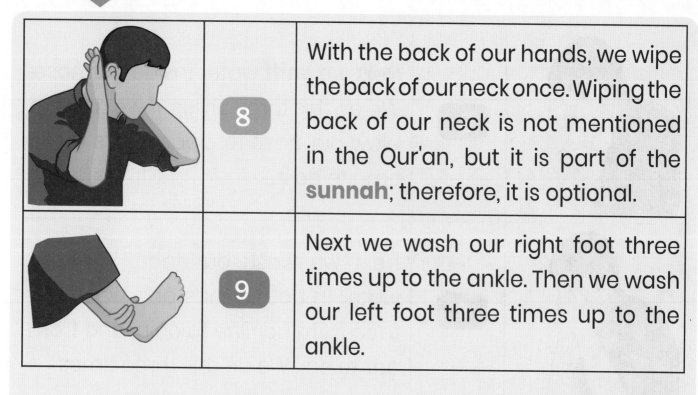

| | | |
|---|---|---|
| | 8 | With the back of our hands, we wipe the back of our neck once. Wiping the back of our neck is not mentioned in the Qur'an, but it is part of the **sunnah**; therefore, it is optional. |
| | 9 | Next we wash our right foot three times up to the ankle. Then we wash our left foot three times up to the ankle. |

Now we are ready to make salah. If you use the toilet, or if you think your wudu has "broken," then you have to make wudu all over again before you can do a salah.

**Words that I learned today:**

Wudu • Sniff • Palms • Sunnah

1. Fill in the blanks using the correct words from the box below.

> salah    hand    head    left

First we wash our right ___hand___, then we wash our
___left___ hand.

We have to make wudu before we do ___salah___.

The sixth step of wudu is to wipe our ___head___.

2. Circle the sentences that are correct. Cross out the sentences that are incorrect.

~~When making wudu, we have to wash our entire body.~~

When making wudu, we have to wash our hair.

~~We can do salah without making wudu.~~

When making wudu, we have to wash our arms.

3. Write four parts of the body that should be cleaned for wudu. The first one is already done for you.

A. ___Hands___          B. ___mouth___

C. ___nose___          D. ___faces___

4. You will need to practice making wudu at home everyday to become perfect. For the next week, mark the times that you practiced making wudu. If you think your wudu was not perfect, mark it with a ⊠. If you think it was perfect, mark it with a ☑.

|           | Fajr | Dhuhr | Asr | Maghrib | 'Isha |
|-----------|------|-------|-----|---------|-------|
| Monday    |      |       |     |         |       |
| Tuesday   |      |       |     |         |       |
| Wednesday |      |       |     |         |       |
| Thursday  |      |       |     |         |       |
| Friday    |      |       |     |         |       |
| Saturday  |      |       |     |         |       |
| Sunday    |      |       |     |         |       |

5. Unscramble the following letters to make meaningful words.

**S A W H**

**T W A R E**    ⬛ ⬛ **T** ⬛ ⬛

**P I W E**

**D U U W**

106

# Unit 3: Messengers of Allah﷾

Throughout the Weekend Learning curriculum, students will learn about the lives and major activities of the messengers. This unit presents the engaging stories of some of the illustrious messengers of Islam. The goal is to capture the imagination of young readers. Whether the lesson focuses on the entire life of a messenger or a specific incident in the messenger's life, these accounts present the narrative true to the Qur'an. The story of Ibrahim (A) is discussed in several levels because there are many moral issues surrounding his interactions with people. The lesson on Yaqub (A) and Yusuf (A) introduces their history. Similarly the lesson on Musa (A) and Harun (S) tell their history. These events will be covered in greater detail in future lessons. The story of Yunus (A) is described in Lesson 16 to highlight the fascinating trials of this nabi. Finally, Lesson 17 provides a summary of life of Nabi Muhammadﷺ, which builds the foundation for many future lessons.

# Unit 3: Messengers of Allah ﷻ

## Ibrahim (A): *A Friend of Allah* ﷻ

While preaching the message of the Oneness of Allāh ﷻ, Ibrahim (A) did some extraordinary things. In this lesson, students will learn some of the ways Ibrahim (A) conveyed this message. He debated with his father and a king. These narratives are fascinating, but they also offer great lesson for students.

## Yaqub (A) and Yusuf (A)

In the narrative of the father and son messengers of Allah ﷻ, we can learn an important lesson about forgiveness. Allah ﷻ says the account of Yusuf (A) is the best story. Students are introduced to the basic events of Yusuf's (A) life. Several chapters will expand upon the outline presented in this chapter.

## Musa (A) and Harun (A)

The lives and activities of Musa (A) and Harun (A) carry great teachings for us. The Qur'an provides many details of their mission. Learning the basic story of their lives now will help students in the future when they study different aspects of these messengers' lives.

## Yunus (A)

In a dramatic manner, Yunus's (A) life suddenly turned from good to bad. These accounts not only include breathtaking suspense, but they also contain great inspiration for us.

## Nabi Muhammad ﷺ

The life of Nabi Muhammad ﷺ cannot be summed up in a few chapters. Throughout the Weekend Learning series, students will learn the different phases and struggles in Nabi Muhammad's ﷺ life. Who was he? Why do we respect him? What exactly did he do? This lesson offers a basic outline of Nabi Muhammad's ﷺ activities.

# Ibrahim (A): *A Friend of Allah*ﷻ

Assalamu alaikum. Welcome to the class. Let us color this sunrise. Ibrahim (A) knew that only Allahﷻ could make the sun rise from the east.

## Ibrahim's (A) belief

Several thousand years ago, a nabi named **Ibrahim** (A) was born in Iraq. Like other nabis and rasuls, he was a brave and honest person. From an early age, Ibrahim (A) believed there is only One God. He did not think idols, plants, animals or planets could be gods.

## Ibrahim's (A) father

Not everyone in Ibrahim's (A) family believed in One God. Ibrahim's (A) father believed in idol gods and worshipped them. One day, Ibrahim (A) asked his father, "O my father! Why do you worship something that does not hear, does not see and does not do anything?"

Ibrahim's (A) point was this: God must be someone who can hear our prayers, who can see us, and who can benefit us. Allahﷻ

is the only God who hears, sees, and benefits us. Therefore, any god other than Allahﷻ is a false god.

Ibrahim's (A) father did not understand this point. Ibrahim (A) told his father that the **idols** he worshipped were not God but Shaitan. Shaitan is Allah'sﷻ enemy. Whoever follows Shaitan will suffer Allah'sﷻ punishment.

His father became so angry that he told Ibrahim (A) to leave the house.

What three things did Ibrahim (A) say idols cannot do?

_can't hear  can't see  won't do any thing_

Worshipping idols is like worshipping _Shaitan_

## Ibrahim (A) and the king

Ibrahim (A) left his hometown. In a new place, Ibrahim (A) began telling people to worship no one but Allahﷻ. His message was plain and simple: There is no god but Allahﷻ.

لَا إِلَهَ إِلَّا اللهُ

A ruler in that country heard that Ibrahim (A) was speaking about God. This made the ruler unhappy. The ruler thought he was God, because he was the most powerful ruler in the kingdom. Ibrahim (A) wanted to make the ruler understand that he was not God. Allah﷾ is God—He gives life and causes death. The ruler thought that if God gives life and causes death, then he is also God, because he can do the same. As a powerful ruler, he can put any person to death or let the person live.

On hearing this, Ibrahim (A) said, "**Allah makes the sun rise from the east. You make the sun rise from the west.**" The ruler realized he could not do it. He realized that he was not God.

## Ibrahim (A) and the idols

One day, Ibrahim (A) went to a temple alone and broke many idols. He wanted people to understand that idols are not God. Later, people saw the idols broken in pieces. Before this, people believed their idols had power. Now they saw the idols could not save themselves. The idols could not even say who broke them. Most people were angry about the broken idols, but a few understood. These few people were **ashamed** for worshipping idols. They understood that idols cannot be gods. The angry people wanted to set Ibrahim (A) on fire to kill him, but Allah﷾ saved him.

What did Ibrahim (A) tell the ruler to do with the sun?
_make thev is sun rise to the west_

What did Ibrahim (A) do in the temple? _break many idols_

## Ibrahim (A) in Egypt

After living in Iraq, Ibrahim (A) went to live in Egypt. He had two sons, **Ismail** (A) and **Ishaq** (A). When both of his sons grew up, they also became nabis of Allah﷾. They all followed the Islamic religion.

Ibrahim (A) also lived in Makkah for some time. Makkah had a structure called the Ka'bah, but it was broken down. Ibrahim (A)

and Ismail (A) put the stones back together to built the Ka'bah. They prayed for everyone to worship only Allah. Allah listened to their prayer. Later, Allah made the Ka'bah our **Qiblah**. This Qiblah is the direction we face for salat.

## Shaitan's tricks

We all know that Shaitan is bad. He wants to trick us to do bad things. One day, Shaitan went up to Ibrahim (A) and Ismail (A). He told them, "Do not listen to Allah!" Do you know what happened next? Ibrahim (A) picked up some rocks and threw them at Shaitan! He threw the rocks to chase away Shaitan.

When people go to Hajj, they throw stones at a certain place to remember Ibrahim's (A) action. They do this to chase away Shaitan from their lives. We do not want Shaitan to be our friend.

**Words that I learned today:**
Ibrahim (A) • Idols • Ashamed • Ismail (A)
Ishaq (A) • Qiblah

1. What are the two ways Ibrahim (A) proved that Allah﷾ was the only God?

he broke the idols and they did nothing. Then Allah saved him

2. Write YES if the sentence is correct. Write NO if it is incorrect.

Ibrahim (A) had two sons who grew up to be nabis.    YES

Ibrahim (A) and Ismail (A) rebuilt the Ka'bah.    YES

Shaitan asked Ibrahim (A) and Ismail (A) to listen to Allah﷾.    NO

Allah﷾ made the Ka'bah the Qiblah because He listened to Ibrahim's (A) prayer.    YES

3. Ask your parents to help you find surah number 14 in the Qur'an. Then write the name of the surah.

Ibrahim

4. Solve the crossword puzzle below.

**Across**:

1. The place where Ibrahim (A) was born.

3. The religion that Ibrahim (A) followed.

4. This prophet was a friend of Allah.

6. Ibrahim's (A) people did not believe in Him.

**Down**:

2. Allah made the Ka'bah our _____

4. Ibrahim (A) broke some of them.

5. This nabi helped his father rebuild the Ka'bah.

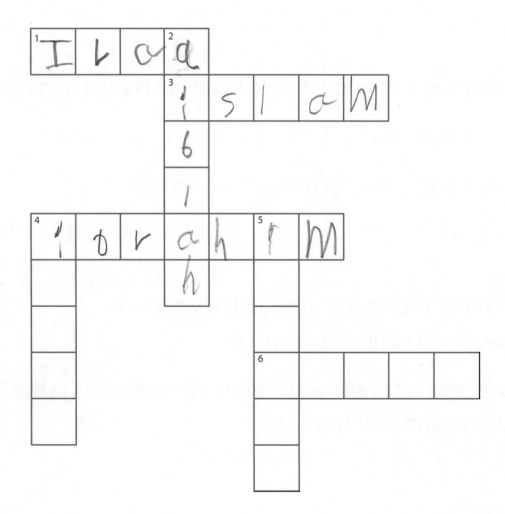

# Yaqub (A) and Yusuf (A)

Assalamu alaikum. Welcome to the class. Let us begin by coloring this deep well in an open field.

## Family history

Previously, we learned that Ibrahim (A) had two sons, Ismail (A) and Ishaq (A). Both sons became nabis of Allahﷻ. When Ishaq (A) grew up, he had a son named **Yaqub** (A). Yaqub (A) was also a nabi of Allahﷻ. Yaqub (A) was Ibrahim's (A) grandson.

When Yaqub (A) grew up, he started a family. He had 12 sons. One of his sons was named **Yusuf** (A). He, too, was a nabi of Allahﷻ. Yusuf (A) was Ibrahim's (A) great-grandson, and Ishaq's (A) grandson.

## Bad brothers

Yaqub (A) loved his youngest son, Yusuf (A), very much. Some of the brothers were jealous that their father loved Yusuf (A). These brothers were bad. They planned to get rid of Yusuf (A). First they

thought they would kill Yusuf (A). Then they decided to drop in a **well**. A well is a deep hole in the ground where you can get water.

One day, the brothers took little Yusuf (A) to a field for a game. Nearby the field was a well. Yusuf's (A) brothers dropped him into the well. Little Yusuf (A) could not climb out of it. The bad brothers went home and told their father that a **wolf** ate Yusuf (A). Yaqub (A) did not believe his sons.

Who was Yusuf's (A) grandfather? Isag

The bad brothers dropped Yusuf (A) in a well

## Yusuf (A) was saved

Sometime later, some people went to the well to get water. They pulled Yusuf (A) out of the well. They took him with them to **Egypt**. There they sold him to a rich family. Although Yusuf (A) was separated from his family, he grew up in a wealthy household.

## Meaning of dreams

Allah ﷻ had given Yusuf (A) knowledge and wisdom. Yusuf (A) became a wise man. He understood the choice between right and wrong. He understood the meanings of dreams.

## King's dreams

One night, the king dreamt about cows and crops. He saw seven large cows eating seven thin cows. Nobody understood the meaning of the dream. But Yusuf (A) was able to tell the meaning.

The king asked Yusuf (A) to work for the kingdom. Yusuf (A) had an important job. He made sure the kingdom had lots of food for years to come.

## Brothers return

After several years, the dry season began. There was no rain, so people could not grow crops. They had no food to eat. Yusuf (A) had stored extra food for the people. Many people from different parts of the country went to Yusuf (A) to get food for their families. People from nearby country also went to Egypt to get food. The bad brothers also went to get some food. They did

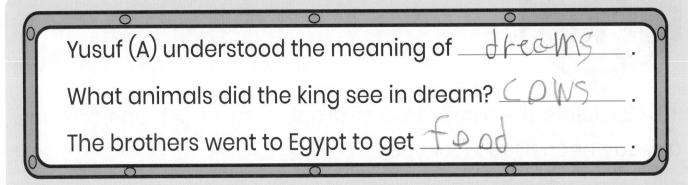

Yusuf (A) understood the meaning of _____dreams_____.

What animals did the king see in dream? _____cows_____.

The brothers went to Egypt to get _____food_____.

not know that their brother, Yusuf (A), was giving out the food. They thought Yusuf (A) had died long ago in the well.

## Family reunites

Yusuf (A) did not tell his brothers who he was at that time. He asked them to bring their youngest brother next time. When the youngest brother came to Egypt, he got into trouble. He was blamed for stealing a valuable cup. Yusuf (A) saved him because he knew his brother did not steal it. Then Yusuf (A) told his brothers his identity. The brothers were sorry for what they had done to Yusuf (A) when he was a child.

Yusuf (A) asked his brothers to bring their father to Egypt. Yusuf (A) was very happy to see his father again after so many years. Allah﷾ is very kind. He **reunited** a father and his beloved son.

**Words that I learned today:**
Yaqub (A) • Yusuf (A) • Well • Wolf • Egypt
Reunited

1. Complete the family tree of prophet Yusuf (A). One box has already been filled in for you.

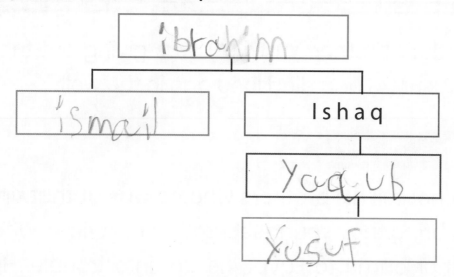

| ibrahim |
| --- |

| ismail | | Ishaq |
| --- | --- | --- |

| Yaqub |
| --- |

| Yusuf |
| --- |

2. Find the following words in the word search puzzle.

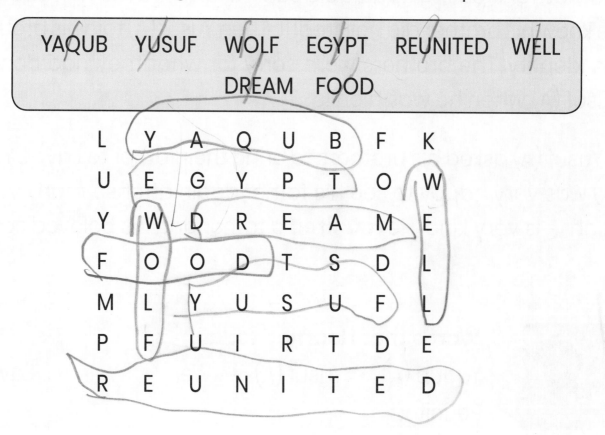

YAQUB   YUSUF   WOLF   EGYPT   REUNITED   WELL

DREAM   FOOD

```
L  Y  A  Q  U  B  F  K
U  E  G  Y  P  T  O  W
Y  W  D  R  E  A  M  E
F  O  O  D  T  S  D  L
M  L  Y  U  S  U  F  L
P  F  U  I  R  T  D  E
R  E  U  N  I  T  E  D
```

3. What did Yusuf's (A) brothers do to him when he was a child?

_throw him in a well_

_____

_____.

4. Write YES if the sentence is correct. Write NO if it is incorrect.

| | |
|---|---|
| Yusuf's (A) brothers told Yaqub (A) that a bear ate Yusuf (A). | No |
| Yusuf (A) grew up in a wealthy family after he was rescued from the well. | yes |
| Yusuf's (A) brothers asked Yusuf (A) for food. | yes |
| Yusuf (A) and Yaqub (A) were reunited after many years. | yes |

5. Ask your parents to help you find surah number 12 in the Qur'an. Then write the name of the surah.

_Surah Yusuf_

# Musa (A) and Harun (A)

Assalamu alaikum. Welcome to the class. Let us color this basket floating in the water.

## Helping the poor

Thousands of years ago a nabi lived in **Egypt**. His name was **Musa** (A). Musa (A) had a brother named **Harun** (A). He was also a nabi. The brothers were from a poor family.

## Pharaoh's fear

In those days, the ruler of Egypt was **Pharaoh**. He was not a good ruler. He was mean to poor people. He did not believe in Allahﷻ. Pharaoh thought he was a god. He was afraid that a boy from one of the poor families would kill him one day. He did not know which boy it would be.  So he ordered all baby boys to be killed. The army began to kill many baby boys.

## Baby Musa (A)

Musa (A) was a baby at that time. His mother became worried. "What will happen to my Musa?" she thought. Allahﷻ told her to place baby Musa (A) in a basket and let him float down the river. She believed Allah﷾ would help Musa (A). She asked her daughter to keep an eye on the basket as it floated down the river. The basket floated slowly until it reached Pharaoh's palace! The queen was surprised and happy to see a baby boy inside the basket. She adopted the boy as her son. Pharaoh could not kill him. Allah﷾ had saved Musa (A).

## A nabi of Allah﷾

When Musa (A) grew up, Allah﷾ made him a nabi. Allah﷾ asked him to help the poor people. Pharaoh made these poor people work as **slaves**. A slave is a person who is forced to work for his or her master and obey the master at all times. Pharaoh made the lives of these slaves very difficult.

Both Musa (A) and Harun (A) went to Pharaoh to tell him about Allahﷻ. They told Pharaoh not to torture the poor people. They asked Pharaoh to free the poor people from their lives as slaves.

> Baby Musa (A) was placed in a ___basket___ on a river.
>
> Pharaoh made the poor people work as ___slaves___ .

## Sign from Allahﷻ

Pharaoh did not believe that Musa (A) was Allah's nabi. He asked Musa (A) to show him a sign from Allahﷻ. Musa (A) threw his stick to the ground and it became a snake. Pharaoh thought it was a **magic** trick He called for some **magicians** to perform better magic. They brought sticks and ropes, which also became snakes. Musa (A) threw his stick again. It became a snake and ate all the other snakes. The magicians believed that Musa (A) was a nabi of Allahﷻ and they became Muslims.

## The slaves are freed

One day, Allahﷻ asked Musa (A) to take the poor people away from Pharaoh. Musa (A) led them to a far-away land. Pharaoh could not stop them from leaving his country. Finally, the poor people were free from slavery.

## Golden cow

After Musa (A) brought the poor people to a safe place, he told Harun (A) to look after them. Musa (A) climbed a mountain to learn more from Allah﷾. While Musa (A) was gone, the people forgot about Allah﷾. They made a cow out of gold and started to worship the cow. Harun (A) told them not to worship anything but Allah﷾. But they became angry with Harun (A). "The cow is our god," they said.

## Musa's (A) reaction

Musa (A) stayed on the mountain for 40 days. During this time, Allah﷾ gave Musa (A) a book. Allah﷾ also taught him **Ten Rules** to follow in daily life. These ten rules are very valuable for all people during all time periods.

When Musa (A) returned from the mountain, he was angry to see the golden cow. He thought his brother, Harun (A), allowed the people to make the cow. But Harun (A) was not responsible for the cow. The people had made the cow by themselves. Musa (A) was unhappy with the people. He told them to worship only Allah. He destroyed the golden cow.

Then the people realized their mistake. They were sorry for their actions. They suffered bad times for worshipping the cow. They began to worship Allah,

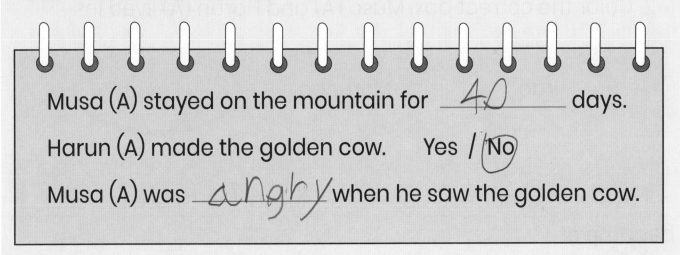

Musa (A) stayed on the mountain for ___40___ days.

Harun (A) made the golden cow.     Yes / No

Musa (A) was ___angry___ when he saw the golden cow.

**Words that I learned today:**

Egypt • Musa (A) • Harun (A) • Pharaoh • Slaves
Magic • Magicians • Ten Rules

Homework

# Weekend 15

1. Color the correct box. Musa (A) and Harun (A) were:

| | | |
|---|---|---|
| Father and son | Two brothers | A king and a magician |

2. Color the correct box. Musa (A) and Harun (A) lived in:

| | | |
|---|---|---|
| Iraq | Morocco | Egypt |

3. Color the correct box. When Musa (A) threw his stick, it became a:

| | | |
|---|---|---|
| Bird | Snake | Camel |

4. Color the correct box. Musa's (A) people worshipped a:

| | | |
|---|---|---|
| Monkey | Bear | Cow |

5. Fill in the blanks using the correct word from the box below.

> queen    40    gold    basket

Musa's (A) mother put baby Musa (A) in a _basket_ .

At the palace, the _queen_ found a baby from the river.

Musa (A) was in a Mountain for _40_ days.

The people worshipped a cow made of _Gold_ .

6. Circle T if the sentence is true. Circle F if the sentence is false.

| Pharaoh made the poor people his slaves. | T F |
| Worshipping a cow is a bad idea. | T F |
| The basket carrying Musa (A) reached Makkah. | T F |
| Harun (A) and the king made a golden cow. | T F |
| The magician's snake ate Musa's (A) stick. | T F |

7. What did the queen do after she picked up baby Musa (A) from the basket on the river?

A. She decided to adopt the baby as her son.

B. She decided to let the baby go.

C. She decided to give the baby to foreigners.

# Yunus (A)

Assalamu alaikum. Welcome to the class. Let us begin by coloring this gourd plant and its large leaves.

## Yunus (A)

A long time ago, there was a place where many bad people lived. They lied, stole, and hurt other people. They did not believe in Allah. To help guide them, Allah sent a nabi. His name was **Yunus** (A).

Yunus (A) told his people to believe in Allah. He tried very hard, but nobody listened to him. He tried again and again, but nobody listened. It seemed like his people would never become good. Yunus (A) became very upset with them.

## Yunus (A) leaves

Yunus (A) did not want to talk to his people anymore. He wanted to go far away from them. He lived near the sea. Yunus (A) thought he could board a ship and go somewhere else. So he left his homeland and boarded a ship.

As the ship sailed on the sea, the weather turned bad. It rained hard. Big waves crashed against the ship. The waves tossed the ship around. The **sailors** became afraid. "Will the ship sink?" they wondered.

The sailors thought that someone on the ship brought them bad luck. They thought that if the person was removed from the ship, then the sea would be safe. The sailors selected a name by holding a **lottery**. In the lottery, they picked Yunus's (A) name!

Then the sailors threw Yunus (A) into the sea! It was a terrifying experience for Yunus (A).

## A whale gulps Yunus (A)

Yunus (A) started to drown in the sea. But Allahﷻ helped him. Allahﷻ sent a big whale to help Yunus (A). The whale gulped him. Yunus (A) entered the whale's body. It was dark and quiet. He prayed to Allahﷻ to forgive him for he had left his homeland without Allah'sﷻ permission.

لَّا إِلَٰهَ إِلَّا أَنتَ سُبْحَٰنَكَ إِنِّي كُنتُ مِنَ ٱلظَّٰلِمِينَ

**La 'Ilaha 'Illa 'Anta Subhanaka 'Inni Kuntu Mina Az-Zalimin.**

This means: **There is no god but You, glory be to You. Surely I became among the unjust.** (21:87)

Let us memorize the dua. Because of this dua, Allahﷻ saved Yunus (A). The whale swam with Yunus (A) inside its body. The

Yunus (A) left his people and boarded a __ship__.

Sailors selected Yunus's (A) name by holding a _lottery_.

A __whale__ gulped Yunus (A) when he was in the sea.

whale came close to the **shore** and left Yunus (A) there. Yunus (A) was very tired. He had been in the rough sea and then inside the body of the whale. Now he was on a lonely, sunny, and very hot beach. He looked for shade, but there was none. He was too weak to walk. So he slept on the burning-hot sand. Then Allah﷾ helped him again. A **gourd** plant grew there and gave him shade with its large leaves.

When Yunus (A) became stronger, he returned to his homeland. He tried once again to tell people about Allah﷾. This time, most people listened to Yunus (A). They started to believe in Allah﷾. Yunus (A) kept trying, and Allah﷾ helped him to become successful.

**Words that I learned today:**

Yunus (A) • Sailors • Lottery • Shore • Gourd

1. Circle T if the sentence is true. Circle F if the sentence is false.

| | |
|---|---|
| Yunus (A) left his town by bus. | T **(F)** |
| The sailors helped Yunus (A) when the weather turned bad. | T **(F)** |
| The ship carrying Yunus (A) sailed in bad weather. | **(T)** F |
| The big whale brought Yunus (A) to shore. | **(T)** F |
| Allah can save you even if you are in a big storm. | **(T)** F |

2. Fill in the blanks using the correct words from the box below.

> tired   sailors   prayed   whale   gourd

A _gourd_ plant has large leaves.

On the shore, Yunus (A) was very _tired_.

Allah sent a big _whale_ to help Yunus (A) after he was thrown into the sea.

Yunus (A) _prayed_ to Allah to forgive him.

The _sailors_ to threw Yunus (A) into the sea.

3. We learn many things from Yunus's (A) life. Write Yes if the sentence is correct. Write No if the sentence is incorrect.

| | |
|---|---|
| Allah﷾ helps us only one time. | No |
| When we try, Allah﷾ helps us. | Yes |
| We should pray only to Allah﷾. | Yes |
| If we cannot solve a math problem, we should try again. | Yes |
| We should give up doing good deeds after doing it once. | No |

4. There are six difference between pictures A and B. Circle the differences.

A

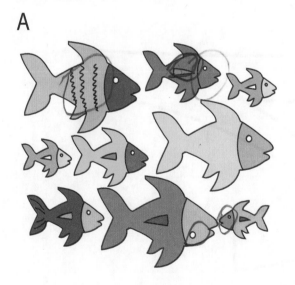

B

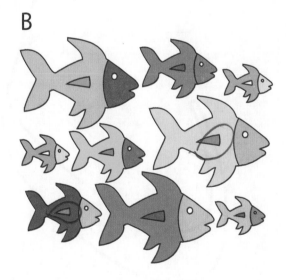

5. Ask your parents to help you find surah number 10 in the Qur'an. Then write the name of the surah.

Yunus

# Nabi Muhammad ﷺ

Assalamu alaikum. Welcome to the class. Let us begin by coloring the Arabic word Muhammad ﷺ.

## Blessing the Nabi ﷺ

Previously we learned that it is common Islamic practice to say a word of glory after Allah's ﷻ name. It is also a common practice to say a word of blessing after Nabi Muhammad's name. We say or write **Sallal-llahu 'alaihi wa Sallam** after his name. It means, "May Allah's Blessings and Peace be upon him." We may write this as (S). In this book, we use the following Arabic blessing word.

**Sallal-llahu 'alaihi wa Sallam**

## Birth of Muhammad ﷺ

About 1,400 years ago, Nabi Muhammad ﷺ was born in **Makkah**, a town in Arabia. His father was named **Abdullah** and his mother was **Aminah**. Abdullah died before Nabi Muhammad ﷺ was born. The year Nabi Muhammad ﷺ was born is known as the **Year of the Elephant**. A Christian ruler went to Makkah with an army and elephants to destroy the Ka'bah. But before he could destroy the Kabah, the army died.

## Early childhood

It was common in Arabia for most newborn babies to be cared for by a **nurse-mother**. A nurse-mother would feed and take care of a baby for several years. Aminah gave her newborn baby, Muhammad ﷺ, to a nurse-mother for a few years. The nurse-mother was very loving. She brought Muhammad ﷺ to her home far away. She took good care of him.

_Abdullah_ was Muhammad's ﷺ father.

Muhammad ﷺ always played with his father.   True / ~~False~~

Aminah sent baby Muhammad ﷺ to a _nurse mother_

## Return to Makkah

A few years later, Nabi Muhammad ﷺ returned to Makkah to live with his mother. At that time, he was five years old. After about a year, Aminah passed away. Nabi Muhammad ﷺ was only **six** years old. His grandfather was very kind and took care

of him for **two** years. Then his grandfather also passed away. Then one of Nabi Muhammad's ﷺ uncle took care of him for several years.

## Truthful and honest

Even in his childhood, Muhammad ﷺ always spoke the truth. People called him **Al-Amin** because they trusted him. He was a truthful and honest person.

When Muhammad ﷺ was a young man, a rich woman named **Khadijah** gave him a job. His job was to buy and sell goods in a far-off place. Muhammad ﷺ took care of her business very well. She was so happy with his work that she married him.

## Rasulullah ﷺ

Many people in Makkah were bad. They were mean to the poor and to women. Muhammad ﷺ did not like this behavior. Every year, he went to a cave to think about these problems. He stayed in the cave for several days.

One year, Muhammad ﷺ was in the cave during Ramadan. One night, angel Jibril (A) came to him with **five** ayat from Allah ﷻ. Muhammad ﷺ became a **Rasulullah**, or a Rasul of Allah. A rasul of Allah ﷻ is a special person who receives Allah's ﷻ message. Over the next 23 years, angel Jibril (A) brought parts of the Qur'an to Muhammad ﷺ.

Nabi Muhammad ﷺ began spreading the message of Islam. He told people about Allah's ﷻ teachings. At first, only a few people believed him and became Muslims. Many people did not believe him. They were mean to him. Some of them even wanted to kill him. Nabi Muhammad ﷺ could not teach Islam in Makkah, so he moved to Madinah. People there loved him very much. He could teach Islam freely in Madinah.

## Trouble in Madinah

When Nabi Muhammad ﷺ was in Madinah, bad people from Makkah went to Madinah to fight the Muslims. They were angry because Nabi Muhammad ﷺ was teaching people about Islam. They fought many battles, but their army could not defeat the Muslim army in any battle.

After many years, Nabi Muhammad ﷺ returned to Makkah. The people in Makkah were afraid. They thought he would punish them for fighting the Muslims. But Nabi Muhammad ﷺ was very kind and forgiving. He did not punish anybody. He forgave everyone in Makkah. The people of Makkah were impressed by his kindness. They accepted Islam and became Muslim.

**Words that I learned today:**
Sallal-Ilahu 'alaihi wa Sallam • Nabi • Abdullah
Aminah • Al-Amin • Khadijah • Rasulullah

1. Color the correct rectangle. Muhammad was called Al-Amin because people:

| Hated him | Trusted him | Feared him |
|-----------|-------------|------------|

2. Color the correct oval. In the Year of the Elephant, Rasulullah was:

Born          Sent to school          Attacked by enemies

3. Color the correct triangle. The Qur'an was sent to Nabi Muhammad over a period of:

23 years          50 years          63 years

4. What does "Sallal-llahu 'alaihi wa Sallam" mean?

may Allah swts blessings and peace be upon him

5. Write four different names or titles for Muhammad ﷺ. These names and titles are in the "Words that I learned today" box.

1. Nabi
2. Rasulullah
3. Al Amin
4. Sallah llahu alaihi wa salam

6. Six events in the life of Nabi Muhammad ﷺ are listed below. These events are not listed in the order they happened. Put the events in the correct order. Write 1 for the first event, 2 for the second event, and so on.

3 | Angel Jibril went to Nabi Muhammad ﷺ.

6 | Nabi Muhammad ﷺ returned to Makkah from Madinah.

2 | Nabi Muhammad ﷺ married Khadijah.

1 | Nabi Muhammad ﷺ was born.

5 | People from Makkah attacked Nabi Muhammad ﷺ in Madinah.

4 | Nabi Muhammad ﷺ moved to Madinah.

# Unit 4: Learning About Islam

The objective of this unit is to introduce students to other aspects of Islam to broaden their knowledge. Many of the concepts discussed in this unit require extensive study. An early understanding of these concepts will help students now and in future grades. The goal here is to keep it simple and enjoyable, yet informative. If students learn just enough of what is presented in each chapter, that will suffice. The concepts introduced here will continue to be covered in greater detail in different grades.

# Unit 4: Learning About Islam

## Obey Allah﷾ and Obey Rasulﷺ

The Qur'ān teaches us to obey Allāh﷾ and obey Rasūlﷺ. This important teaching is presented to students through a story of a team of players winning a soccer game. Their win became possible because they trained under a coach and obeyed him. Similarly, in our daily lives, we can be successful if we train under the guidance of Allāh﷾ and obey His teaching and obey our Rasūlﷺ, who is like our coach.

## Day of Judgment

Belief in the Day of Judgment is an important part of our faith. A large part of the Qur'an focuses on the concept of Judgment Day and Akhirat. This chapter introduces students to the key events on this Day. The idea is not to scare them with the gravity of the event, but to educate them in a manner that is best for their age and guiding them to prepare for this day.

## Our Masjid

This lesson uses a story of two young boys who become friends. Together they explore their masjid. They demonstrate how small actions by each person can bring about a nice improvement in the maintenance of their masjid. The story teaches students how they can take care of their masjid.

## Islamic Phrases

In this chapter, students will read some common Islamic phrases that people use in their daily lives. They will learn the meaning of these phrases and the specific occasions when they are used.

## Food That We May Eat

Islam has very detailed dietary laws. This lesson introduces students to the concepts of halal and haram, and teaches them the types of food that are halal and haram. Understanding these dietary laws will help students avoid prohibited food.

# Obey Allah ﷻ, Obey Rasul ﷺ

Assalamu alaikum. Welcome to the class. Let us begin by coloring the soccer ball.

## A soccer game

"Goal!" screamed the parents and kids of Pebble Brook Elementary. In a few minutes, they screamed again. "Goal!"

By the time the soccer game was over, the second graders of Pebble Brook had beaten Boulder Creek Elementary 6–0. Sharif, alone, had scored four goals. Arif, could not stop smiling. Arif is a high-school student and the soccer coach at Pebble Brook.

## Following the rules

Sharif recalled his last three months of **training** under Arif. It was fun even though Arif had many rules. He was strict but not mean. Everyone had to arrive at the soccer field by 4 pm. He made sure there was discipline on the soccer field. He gave the players rules on how to pass the ball, how to run with the ball, and how to score a goal. He set specific times for breaks and for the end of practice.

Arif had a specific rule during summer soccer practice. At 6 pm, Arif would stop the practice and say: "Muslim kids, join me for Asr salat. Other kids, please take a break and think or do something good!" There were four Muslim kids on Pebble Brook's second-grade soccer team. All of them stood behind Arif to pray four rakah of Asr salat.

## Allah's rule

Mujib, a player on the soccer team, asked Arif, "Is the prayer also a rule, Boss?" Arif smiled. "No, prayer is not my rule. This is Allah's rule. If we **obey** Allah and His Rasul, then we will have a good life in this world and in the **afterlife**. When you listen to me, you will play well against Boulder Creek. When you listen to Allah and His Rasul, everything will be very good in your life."

"But I don't know how to listen to Allah and His Rasul," said Mujib. "And how can I listen to Rasulullah?"

After practice, the Muslim kids sat near Arif to learn how to obey Allah and His Rasul. Arif said, "We are Muslims because we believe in Allah, who is the only God. We also believe that Muhammad is Allah's rasul and the final nabi."

"We learned '**La ilaha illa llahu Muhammadur Rasulullah.**' This means there is no one to worship except Allah, and Muhammad is His Rasul. I repeat this every day."

Arif said. "Let me teach you part of an ayat today. In the Qur'an, there is a surah, or chapter, called An-Nur. One part of the surah says, "Obey Allah and obey the Rasul. In Arabic, we say, "**Atiullahu wa atiur rasul.**"

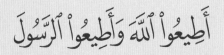

## Meaning of obey

Arif explained, "Obey means to follow an order. When you obey someone, you do what the person asks you to do. When we obey Allah﷾, we do what Allah﷾ told us to do. We don't do anything that Allah﷾ doesn't want us to do. We obey Allah's﷾ rules."

## Allah's﷾ rules

Arif continued, "Allah﷾ has many rules, and they are in the Qur'an. There are rules about how to live our lives, how to behave with others, how to earn and spend money, and how to pray to Allah﷾. If we follow Allah's﷾ rules, we obey Him. It's good for everyone to follow Allah's﷾ rules."

## How to obey Rasulullah?

Arif explained. "About 1400 years ago, Allah﷾ sent Rasulullahﷺ to show us how to practice our religion. Rasulullahﷺ is our guide and teacher. He taught us the best way to do things in our lives. He showed us how to pray and how to fast. We obey his way of praying and fasting. He also showed us how to treat others. He showed us what to do when we face problems. And he explained what we should not do. When we learn more about his life, we learn how to obey him."

Then Arif added, "There are other ayats in the Qur'an that also say we should obey Allah﷾ and obey the rasulﷺ. This rule is repeated because it's important. Can anyone say this verse in Arabic?"

Another player, Nayeem, quickly said, "I have already learned it—I know it by heart. It's 'Atiullahu wa atiur rasul,' from Surah An-Nur." Then Rauf said, "I know it by heart, too. 'Atiullahu wa atiur rasul.'"

Arif explained, "There was no soccer when Rasulullah(S) was alive. But...we can use his teachings anywhere—in our schools, workplaces, stores, and even soccer fields. Rasulullah(S) taught us to be fair, to be kind to others, and to never cheat. In our games, we will play hard, but we will be nice to other teams. And we will not cheat."

 **Words that I learned today:**
Training • Obey • Afterlife • Atiul-llaha wa atirur Rasul

1. The word "obey" means:

   A.   To play a soccer game nicely

   B.   To follow someone's orders

   C.   To make your own rules

   D.   To work hard in your studies

2. Circle C if the sentence is correct. Circle W if the sentence is wrong.

When we obey Allah, we are nice to others.          (C)   W

When we obey Allah, our lives become better.        (C)   W

When we obey Allah, we are mean to others.          C   (W)

When we obey Allah, we pray regularly.              (C)   W

3. Why should we obey Rasulullah?

   A.   Because Arif told the players to obey Rasulullah.

   B.   Because Allah told us to obey Rasulullah.

   C.   Because we can win a soccer game.

   D.   Because Rasulullah was born 1,400 years ago.

# Day of Judgment

Assalamu alaikum. Welcome to the class. Let us color these fallen leaves. Like the leaves and the seasons, the world will end one day, too.

## Everything will end

Allah﷾ is the Creator of everything. Everything that He created will come to an end one day. During the Spring, trees are full of leaves. In Autumn, the leaves fall and die. Today, billions of people live on Earth. One day, all the people will also die. Nobody can live forever. The world will not exist forever, either. Only Allah﷾ lives **forever**.

## Articles of faith

Our faith, or **Iman**, teaches us many things about Islam. There are six articles of Iman. These six articles are: (1) belief in Allah﷾, (2) belief in the angels, (3) belief in the books, (4) belief in the rasuls, (5) belief in the **Akhirat**, (6) belief in the will of Allah﷾, and (7) belief in the **Awakening**.

## What is Akhirat?

Islam teaches us that we live in this world and in the **Akhirat**. The word Akhirat simply means "life after our death." This new life does not start immediately after we die. In the future, a day will come when all living beings will die. Everything on the earth will be destroyed. This day is called the **Last Day**. Next, all dead people will be alive again. Then a new period of time will begin. This new period is the Akhirat

of Hereafter. Many things will happen during the Akhirat. The **Day of Judgment** is the most important event in the Akhirat.

## Day of Judgment

After everything on Earth is destroyed, Allah﷾ will bring all the dead people back to life. The Day of Judgment will begin. On the Judgment Day, Allah﷾ will judge good people and bad people. Allah﷾ is the best Judge. He will judge all our **deeds**, large and small. Nobody will be able to hide anything from Allah﷾.

## Scale of deeds

On Judgment Day, our deeds will be weighed on a **scale**. If we did more good deeds than bad deeds on earth, our scale will be heavy. We will go to **Heaven**. If our scale is light, it will be bad for us.

## Witness

Allah﷾ will call for a **witness**. A witness is someone or something that saw us doing a good or bad thing. Our bodies and known people will reveal if we did good or bad deeds. Nobody will help us if we did not do good things in this world. If we do good deeds, then we do not have to worry about a witness.

## Good and bad people

The good people will have bright and happy faces. They will have nothing to fear. They will go to Heaven. The bad people will have dark and sad faces. They will be very sad and ashamed that they did not follow Allah's teachings. They will want to return to Earth to do good deeds. But they will not be given another chance.

After Judgment Day, Allah will discipline the bad people. He will reward those who performed good deeds on Earth. He will reward those who believed in Him. All good people will receive their own rewards. No one can take away our rewards.

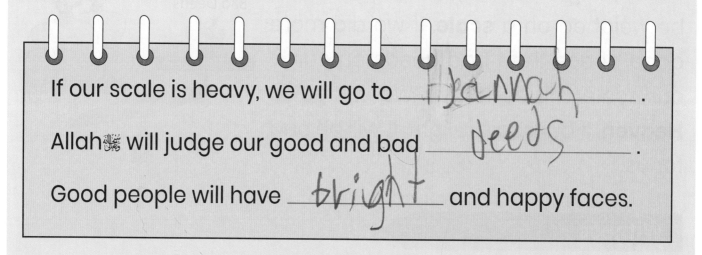

If our scale is heavy, we will go to ___Hannah___.

Allah will judge our good and bad ___deeds___.

Good people will have ___bright___ and happy faces.

On Judgment Day, there will be three types of people. The best people will receive the best rewards. The good people will be in another group, and they will receive good rewards. The last group of people will be the bad ones. They will not get any rewards. They will suffer punishment.

## Life in the Akhirat

When the Day of Judgment ends, we will begin our life in the Akhirat. Our life on earth is short. But life in the Hereafter will last forever.

Allah tells us that life in the Hereafter is real. We do not know much about that life. We cannot completely understand how good that life will be. The Qur'an says the Hereafter will be better than anything we can imagine!

If we are good Muslims, Allah will reward us with good things. The good people will be in **Jannah**, which is a beautiful Garden. This is a place of peace. Children will be with their parents and other family members in Jannah. We only have to be good Muslims to have a wonderful life in Jannah.

**Words that I learned today:**
Forever • Iman • Akhirat • Awakening • Scale
Deeds • Day of Judgment • Witness • Jannah

1. Find the following words in the word search puzzle.

FOREVER  JUDGMENT  SCALE  JANNAH  EARTH  REWARD  LIFE

```
B  E  A  R  T  H  J  A
S  P  E  R  S  B  U  N
A  T  J  E  C  W  D  W
C  L  X  W  A  R  G  P
L  I  A  A  L  F  M  R
S  F  O  R  E  V  E  R
T  E  Q  D  O  A  N  X
J  A  N  N  A  H  T  G
```

2. There will be three types of people on the Judgment Day.
Write the three types of people in the boxes below.

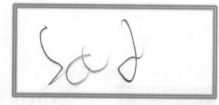

3. Our good deeds and bad deeds be weighed on a: Scale

**158**

4. Circle T if the sentence is true. Circle F if the sentence is false.

| | | |
|---|---|---|
| On the Judgment Day, Allah ﷻ will reward all the good people. | **T** | F |
| The Judgment Day happens once every year. | T | **F** |
| Bad people will receive rewards on Judgment Day. | T | **F** |
| Life in the Hereafter will last for only a few years. | T | **F** |
| The good people will enter Jannah, a beautiful Garden. | **T** | F |
| On Judgment Day, friends cannot help another friend. | **T** | F |

5. To receive good rewards in the Hereafter, what should we do now?

do good deeds

# Our Masjid

Assalamu alaikum. Can you color this Masjid? This Masjid is in India.

## Arriving in masjid

Sajid and Samira could hear the adhan call when their father pulled into the masjid parking lot. It seemed like they were a little late for Maghrib salat. The parking lot was covered with recent snow.

By the time Sajid and Samira entered the masjid, their boots were wet and covered with snow. Sajid and Samira quietly and neatly placed their boots on the shoe rack. They made sure not to get the carpet wet in the masjid.

## A friend in the masjid

After Sajid finished his salat, he saw a new boy who had also finished his salat. Sajid walked over to him. "Assalamu Alaikum. My name is Sajid. Are you new to our masjid?"

The new boy replied, "Walaikum Salam. Yes, I'm new. My name is Khaled. We just moved here from California." Sajid ofered to walk him around the masjid.

Sajid and Khaled lowered their voices as some people were still praying. Sajid told Khaled that they always keep the salat area very clean. "This is an area to remember Allah, so nobody talks loudly in the large hall. The only person who may talk loudly is the Imam when he gives a **khutbah** or leads a salat or a **halaqa**."

Some of the families started to quietly leave the masjid. Then Sajid said, "We can't run around in the salat area." Khaled replied, "It was like that in our old masjid. We never ran around in the masjid. We weren't allowed to walk in front of someone who was praying."

## Wudu area in masjid

Sajid took Khaled to the men's wudu area first. Khaled noticed one **faucet** was dripping water. He turned off the faucet.

As they were leaving the wudu area, they saw two wet flip-flops on the floor. Khaled picked them up and put them on the rack. "Now they can dry before the next salat," said Khaled.

## Library in masjid

Next, Sajid offered to show Khaled the library. They walked down the hallway to a room with large desks and many shelves full of books. Only one person was in the library. Khaled and Sajid greeted him. "Assalamu alaikum." The man replied, "Walaikum salam, children!"

They looked through some books in the children's section. Sajid wanted to show Khaled another place before dinner. As they left the library, they turned off the lights because no one else was in the library.

Down the hall, they opened the door to another room. Khaled saw a basketball court. Sajid said, "Khaled, you know we can't talk loudly or run around in the salat hall or in the library, but we can play as much as we want here." Sajid threw a basketball to Khaled.

Khaled dribbled the ball and then threw it in the basket. On the other side of the room, there were three tall kids who were also playing basketball. They looked like high-school kids. Khaled said, "Insha Allah, I will be as tall as them in a few years, and almost touch the basket." They played basketball until the older kids left the court.

## Dining hall

After playing basketball, two friends walked to the dining hall. There was already a long line. Khaled and Sajid waited at the end of the long line. They were hungry. They hoped the pizza did not run out before they reached the table. After a few minutes, which seemed like an hour, they reached the table.

Sajid was happy to see there was still some warm pizza on the table. He said, "Khaled, I'm so hungry! I'm gonna take five slices of the pizza! I could eat a mountain!"

"No, you cannot," said Khaled. "And not five slices. Just pick two. That might be enough. If you're still hungry, you can get more later or eat something else."

Khaled chose some biryani rice and pasta. "Pasta will make my biryani less spicy." They both laughed.

## Helping in dining room

They put their plates on a table and greeted the people already sitting there. Then they walked over to the beverage area. Sajid picked up a water bottle. Khaled picked up four bottles. "I'm going to give water to the other people at the table. Being good to others is a **sadaqa**." On hearing this, Sajid also picked up four bottles.

The people were happy to receive the water bottles. They said, "**Jazakumullahu khairan**."

Khaled and Sajid were happy that other people made a dua, or prayer, for them. After they sat down, they said "Bismillah" before taking their first bite. They know they should start any meal or work in the name of Allah.

After finishing, Khaled and Sajid took the empty plates to the garbage cans. They saw the older kids from the basketball court taking some garbage bags to the outdoor trash containers.

Khaled and Sajid quickly picked up the empty water bottles from their table and put them in the recycling bins.

"Yes, let's clean up the tables." In a few minutes, the dining hall was clean and tidy. Khaled and Sajid were happy about their good deed.

Then it was time to go home. In the parking lot, they met the Imam and greeted him with a salam. They asked the Imam to make a dua for them. The Imam is a gentle and kind man. He smiled. "Insha Allah, I will make a dua for you. Please also make a dua on your own."

Sajid is happy today. He knows he found a good friend. "Khaled, I'm going to pray Isha at home tonight. Insha Allah, I'll be back for Maghrib salat tomorrow. If you're here tomorrow, I'll introduce you to my other friends."

"Insha Allah," Khaled replied. He is also happy to find a good friend. He knows that he will help keep his new masjid nice and clean.

**Words that I learned today:**
Khutbah • Halaqa • faucet • Sadaqa
Jazakulullahu Khairan

1. Cross out the acts that we should NOT do in the masjid.

   a. Talk loudly while others are praying.

   b. Make the masjid dirty.

   c. Walk in front of people when they are praying.

   d. Keep shoes on the shoe rack.

   e. Listen to the Imam while he is talking.

2. What should we say before we begin any work?

   bismillah

3. When we want something to happen in the future, what should we say? inshallah

4. Circle all correct answers. What is an example of good table manners?

   a. Taking only the food that you can eat.

   b. Keeping your table clean.

   c. Helping others get food or water.

   d. Going to the front of the line if you're really hungry.

5. Circle all the correct answers. What is an example of good manners in the wudu room?

   a. Turning off the faucet after making wudu.

   b. Keeping the floor of the wudu room dry.

   c. Keeping flip-flops on the rack.

   d. Trying to reach the masjid with wudu.

   e. Wearing flip-flops to the salat hall.

6. Circle all the correct answers. What is an example of good manners after you finish your dinner?

   a. Saying "Alhamdulillah."

   b. Leaving plates, forks, and spoons on the table.

   c. Putting waste in the garbage bin.

   d. Never putting anything in the recycling bin.

   e. Helping others clean up.

# Islamic Phrases

Assalamu alaikum. Let us begin by coloring the phrase, "Bismillahir Rahmanir Rahim." Remember to say, "Bismillah" before you begin coloring.

## Common Islamic phrases

A **phrase** is a word or a small group of words. An Islamic phrase is word or a small group of words that have some meaning. A common Islamic phrase is "**Allahu Akbar**." It means "Allah is Greater." Here, "Allahu" is a word and "Akbar" is another word. They join together to make a phrase.

Every language has a large number of common phrases. For example, the greeting "Good Morning" is a phrase. The expression "Thank you" is a phrase.

In Islam, there is a large number of phrases that people use regularly. Let us learn some of these common phrases.

## Allahu Akbar

Previously we mentioned, Allahu Akbar is a common Islamic phrase.

$$اللّٰهُ أَكْبَر$$

We use this phrase anytime good work is done. We say it several times during our salat. We say it before or after doing a good deed. It is a reminder that Allah﷾ is in control of everything we do. We also use the phrase as a dua to seek Allah's﷾ approval for good work. Allah﷾ never likes bad deeds. Therefore, we should never say it while doing something bad.

## Bismillah

Another common Islamic phrase is "Bismillahir-Rahmani-r Rahim." The short form of this phrase is "**Bismillah**."

We should remember Allah when we begin any work. The best way to remember Allah﷾ is to say, "Bismillah" before we do any work. When we say "Bismillah," we seek Allah's﷾ blessings.

بِسْمِ ٱللَّهِ ٱلرَّحْمَٰنِ ٱلرَّحِيمِ ۝

**Bismillahir-Rahmani-r-Rahim**

It means: "In the name of Allah, most Beneficial, most Merciful."

## Al-Hamdulillah

Another common phrase in Islam is, "Al-Hamdulillah."

ٱلْحَمْدُ لِلَّهِ

The phrase means, "All praise be to Allah." We say it to give thanks to Allah. When we say al-Hamdulillah, we **glorify** Allah﷾ and show that everything that happens to us is due to Allah's﷾ mercy. We use this phrase after finishing good work, after we hear good news, or when we feel good about anything.

## Insha-Allah

We often use the phrase, "insha-Allah." Nothing in this world happens without permission from Allah﷾. If Allah﷾ does not want something to happen, it will not happen. We should make it a habit to say "insha-Allah" when we plan to do anything later today, tomorrow, or in the future. The phrase means, "If Allah wants."

إِن شَآءَ ٱللَّه

**Insha-Allah**

## Ma-Sha-Allah

Another common phrase we say is "Ma-Sha-Allah."

مَاشَآءَ ٱللَّه

It means, "as Allah wanted." We use this phrase to express our thanks and joy for something that has **already** happened. For example, "Your house is beautiful, ma-Sha-Allah," or "that birthday celebration was wonderful, ma-Sha-Allah."

## Astaghfirul-Ilah

Sometimes we knowingly or unknowingly make a mistake. We do something wrong to others or to ourselves. So we say, "Astaghfirul-Ilah." It means, "I seek forgiveness from Allah."

أَسْتَغْفِرُواْ ٱللَّه

We should say, "astaghfirul-Ilah" as often as we can, because we do not always know when we have made a mistake.

## Baraka-Ilahu

We often say, "Baraka-Ilahu fik" or simply, "Baraka-Ilahu." It means, "Blessings of Allah﷾ be upon you."

$$بَارَكَ ٱللَّهُ فِيكَ$$

**Baraka-Ilahu fik**

We use this phrase to express thanks to another person. We do not use this phrase to thank Allah﷾.

## Subhana-Ilah

Another common phase in Islam is "Subhana-Ilah." It means, "Glory to Allah." This phrase is used to indicate amazement at Allah's﷾ creations or to His qualities. Instead of saying "Wow!" at something, we might say, "Subhaha-Ilah," to express our wonder.

$$سُبْحَانَ ٱللَّه$$

**Subhana-Ilah**

**Words that I learned today:**

Phrase • Allahu Akbar • Bismillah • Al-Hamdulillah Glorify • Insha-Allah • Ma-Sha-Allah • Astaghfirul-llah • Baraka-Ilahu fik • Subhana-Ilah

1. Before we do good work, what phrase should we say?

    A. Allahu-Alam.

    B. Allahu-Akbar.

    C. Allahu-s-Samad.

2. When we plan to do something at a later time, what phrase should we use to show our trust in Allahﷻ?

    A. Allahu-Akbar.

    B. Ma-Sha Allah.

    C. Insha-Allah.

3. When we want to thank a person, what phrase should we say?

    A. Al-Hamdulillah.

    B. Baraka-llahu Fik.

    C. Astaghfirul-llah.

4. What phrase should we use to ask for Allah'sﷻ forgiveness?

# Food That We May Eat

Assalamu alaikum. Today we will color this dinner plate. Allah ﷻ has given us so much good food.

## Halal and haram food

Allahﷻ has given us many different kinds of food. All these foods are gifts from Allahﷻ. He has also given us certain rules about eating food.

Allahﷻ allows us to eat all good and pure food. These are called **halal** foods. There are other foods that Allahﷻ does not want us to eat. These are called **haram** foods.

## Good practice

Not all food available in the grocery store is halal for us. Muslims should be very careful to choose only halal food to eat. Before we eat any food, we should say, "*Bismillahir Rahmanir Rahim.*" We should remember Allahﷻ, and thank Him for His gifts to us. We should not waste our food.

## Fruits and vegetables

Allahﷻ allows us to eat all fruits, vegetables and edible grains. Fruits, vegetables and grains are halal. However, some fruits

and vegetables are poisonous or harmful if taken. For example, **tobacco** leaves and their products can be harmful. Some nuts are poisonous for certain people. Some fruits and vegetables might have too many harmful chemicals in them. If we know certain foods or plants are harmful, we should avoid them.

## Halal and Haram meat

Some meats are halal, and some are haram. Halal meats are from good animals, such as cows, lambs, and chickens. In order for meat to be halal, the meat of these animals is prepared in an **Islamic** way by remembering Allahﷻ. The Islamic way of killing an animal and preparing its meat is called **Zabiha**.

The Qur'an says that sometimes the meat of animals, such as cows, lambs, and chickens can be harmful for us. We should be careful not to eat harmful meat. For example, we should avoid diseased cows and rotten meat.

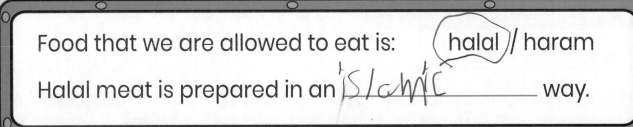

Food that we are allowed to eat is: (halal) / haram

Halal meat is prepared in an _Islamic_ way.

The meat of a pig is haram. As Muslims, we do not eat any meat from pigs. These meats might be called **pork**, **ham**, **sausage**, or **bacon**. We do not eat any of these meats. Before we eat any boxed or canned food, it is a good idea to check the list of **ingredients**. If we see any pork ingredients, we should not eat that food.

## Fish is halal

The Qur'an says that all living creatures in the water are halal. All fish from oceans, lakes, and rivers are halal to eat. However, some fish might be poisonous or harmful if eaten. Therefore, we should use caution before we eat them.

## Drinks and juices

There are many varieties of drinks and juices on the market. Not all drinks and juices are good for us. A large variety of **wine**, **liquor**, and **beer** is available. These drinks contain **alcohol**. Muslims are not allowed to drink alcohol.

## Only good food

Allah﷾ wants us to eat only good food. We should not eat haram food, rotten food or food that is not good for us. We should also not waste food. It is not healthy to eat too much or too little.

We can eat food made by Christians and Jews if the food is halal. If we know that a food was offered to an idol or a false god, then we cannot eat that food.

When we finish eating, we should thank Allah﷾ for His gifts to us. We should say, "Al-hamdulillah."

**Words that I learned today:**
Halal • Haram • Zabiha • Pork • Ham • Sausage
Bacon • Ingredients • Wine • Beer • Alcohol

1. Write in the circles five kinds of food that Muslims should not eat.

1.

vine

2.

Allahol

3.

bacon

4.
pork
Pork

5.

beer

2. What should we say before we eat any food?

_Bismilah hel rrahmanerahem_

3. Let us write some antonyms (words that have opposite meanings). One is already done for you.

| Good | Bad |
|------|-----|
| Halal | Haram |
| Hard | easy |
| Haram | Halal |

4. Color the correct box. Zabiha is the proper way of:

| Washing a fish | Killing an animal for food | Making juice |
|---|---|---|

5. Color the correct box. Before we buy boxed or canned food, we should look at the:

List of ingredients    Picture of animals    Color of the box or can

6. Color the correct box. We should read the list of ingredients to see if the food has:

| Hidden gifts | Haram items | Puzzles |
|---|---|---|

7. We should not waste good halal food. Pretend you are at a friend's house and someone gives you a sandwich. It has bacon on it! What should you do?

Tell them you cannot eat bacon and say it is haram.

# Unit 5: Akhlaq and Adab in Islam

These lessons focus on proper Islamic manners and moral issues. Good moral conduct does not make a person suffer; it helps one to become better in the sight of humanity and God. Akhlaq (Morality) and Adab (Manners) are two important areas of learning in Islam. Proper akhalq and adab require knowing and demonstrating these concepts and practices in everyday life. It is not simply an individual commitment; it is also a collective commitment. A traditional understanding of akhlaq and adab has universal appeal and has stood the test of time. The teachings of the Qur'an and authentic sunnah are the best. Throughout the entire Weekend Learning series, several areas of ideal human behavior will be emphasized. Students should learn this ideal behavior and practice it in their daily lives

Lesson 23:     Truthfulness

Lesson 24:     Kindness

Lesson 25:     Respect

Lesson 26:     Responsibility

Lesson 27:     Obedience

Lesson 28:     Cleanliness

Lesson 29:     Honesty

# Unit 4: Akhlaq and Adab in Islam

## Truthfulness

Students are taught the value of truthfulness in life. They should learn to speak the truth and realize the rewards for being truthful in life. The sooner students learn the importance of truthfulness, the sooner they will adopt this value.

## Kindness

Sometimes the world can be very unkind to us. How do we live in an unkind world but show kindness toward everyone and everything? Islam teaches us to adopt kindness toward everything around us. Kindness teaches students not to be selfish and not to be oblivious to the world around them.

## Respect

This lesson teaches students the importance of showing respect to the people around them. They will also learn how to properly show respect.

## Responsibility

In this chapter, students are introduced to the value of responsibility. How can responsibility make a person successful in life? How can an irresponsible life jeopardize a person? Students will learn the importance of being responsible regarding different matters in life. This is one of the values that makes an ordinary person successful in life.

## Obedience

Islam requires us to show obedience to Allahﷻ and our Rasulﷺ. There are other forms of obedience that are also important. Obedience is one of the character traits that makes a person a good individual.

## Cleanliness

The cleanliness of our bodies, minds, and surrounding environment is important for healthy living. Islam emphasizes that cleanliness be maintained in all aspects of life. This lesson introduces the basics of how we can maintain cleanliness.

## Honesty

Honesty and truthfulness go hand in hand. If truthfulness is about speaking the truth, then honesty is about behaving in a truthful manner. Our everyday life offers plenty of opportunities to display honesty or dishonesty. An early understanding of the value of honesty will help shape the lives of students in an ideal manner.

# Truthfulness

Assalamu alaikum. Welcome to the class. Let us color Tahira, who is doing her homework. She always does her homework on time.

## Truthful

Every day, we should try to be **truthful**. This means that we should speak the truth and behave in the correct manner. If we do not speak the truth, then we are lying. Allahﷻ does not love people who lie. He loves those who speak the truth.

## Nabis were truthful

We can learn many good things from the life of our Nabi Muhammadﷺ. He always spoke the truth, even before he became a rasul. Rasulullahﷺ was truthful all his life. He never lied. He was truthful in his words and his actions. Because of his nature, people loved him and trusted him. The people of Makkah called him **Al-Amin**, the **trustworthy**.

All the nabis and rasuls were also truthful people. We already read about Ibrahim (A), Yaqub (A), Yusuf (A), Musa (A), and Yunus (A) in this book. They had many difficulties in their lives, but they never lied or failed to tell the truth.

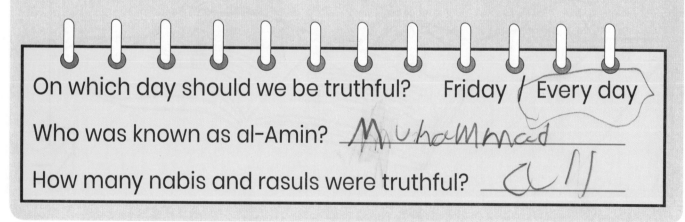

On which day should we be truthful?    Friday / Every day

Who was known as al-Amin? _Muhammad_

How many nabis and rasuls were truthful? _الله_

## Which one is better?

Nabis and rasuls faced difficulties for being truthful. Does this mean truth brings difficulties in life? No. Actually lies bring problems in life. In fact, lies bring more **trouble** than truth. Truth makes you become a strong person. Truth brings success in life. Truth brings peace in life. Allah﷾ loves truth, therefore, He makes truthful people happy in life.

Lies make a person's life sad and miserable. A liar is like a mouse—always trying to hide, because the lies can be caught at any moment. We do not want to be like a mouse. We want to speak the truth, because there is no fear of getting caught.

## Allah knows what you say

A person who does not speak the truth forgets about Allah﷾. The person thinks nobody will know if he or she is lying. Allah﷾ always knows who speaks the truth and who does not. We cannot hide anything from Him. If we tell a lie, our parents and teachers can often find out. It is never a good idea to tell lies.

If we do good things, then we can always speak the truth. People lie when they do bad things. If you do your homework on time, then you do not have to make up a story. Making up a story is lying. In the picture on the first page of this lesson, Tahira is doing her homework on time, so she does not need to make up a story.

## Rewards from Allah

Many verses in the Qur'an say that Allah will bless and reward the truthful people. These people will live in Paradise. Many hadith of Rasulullah remind us to be truthful. One hadith teaches us that if we are truthful, then we can go to Heaven.

Your parents will be happier if you speak the truth. Your teacher and friends will like you if you always speak the truth.

Allah tells us to speak the truth. Shaitan tells us to lie. We should not listen to Shaitan. He is not our friend. Shaitan wants us to get into trouble. When we lie, we get into trouble. Shaitan becomes happy when we get into trouble.

If we do something bad, we should not try to cover it up with lies. We should say we are sorry to Allah. Saying we are sorry to Allah means that we make **tawbah**. Allah is very kind and forgives us when we make tawbah.

## Words that I learned today:
Truthful • Al-Amin • Trustworthy • Trouble
Tawbah

1. What does it mean to be truthful?

_____

_____

2. Write a few rewards that we receive for being truthful.

A. _____

B. _____

C. _____

3. Who tells us to speak the truth?

_____

4. Who tells us to lie?

_____

5. Where will the truthful people be after they die?

_____

6. Arrange these jumbled letters into meaningful words.

HTRTU    ☐ ☐ ☐ **T** ☐

LA MAIN    ☐ ☐ **A** ☐ ☐

RRWADE    **R** ☐ ☐ **R** ☐

7. Fill in the blanks using the correct word from the box below.

| listen | truth | friend | lie | happy | trouble |

Allahﷻ tells us to speak the _____ .

Shaitan tells us to _____ .

We should not _____ to Shaitan. He is not our

_____ .

Shaitan wants us to get into _____ .

When we get into trouble, Shaitan becomes _____ .

# Kindness

Assalamu alaikum. Welcome to the class. Let us color this picture of little Asma. She is a kind girl who loves to feed hungry birds.

**24**

## Kindness

You show **kindness** whenever you help or support someone. Kindness means being nice to others. We are kind when we make things easy for others. This means that if we do something that makes another person feel good, then it is an act of kindness.

When we are kind, it not only makes us feel good—it also makes another person feel good.

## Many ways to be kind

We should be kind to people who are younger than us. We should also be kind to those who are older than us. We can show kindness in many ways. When we smile at someone, we are being kind to him or her. When we **praise** someone for doing good work, we are being kind. If we give someone a hug, we are being kind. When we do not hurt others' feelings, we are being kind to them. When we say *salam* to someone, we are being kind.

Kindness touches others and makes their day brighter. Kindness is like sunshine—it warms up everything. Have you been kind to someone today?

## Kind to everything

A good Muslim is kind to people, animals, and plants. We should be kind to poor and needy people. We should not hurt an animal for fun. We should not pluck plants or flowers just for fun.

When Nabi Muhammadﷺ and the Muslims lived in Madinah, the **idol worshippers** fought them. When the Nabiﷺ returned to Makkah as the winner, he was very kind. He did not punish the idol worshippers; he forgave them. This was a great act of kindness. The idol worshippers were won over by his kindness. They became Muslims.

## Surah Ma'un

The Qur'an has a surah called *Al-Ma'un,* or **Acts of Kindness**. In this surah, Allahﷻ tells us to be kind to orphans and the poor. Allahﷻ tells us that some people do salat only to show others, and they are unmindful. They fail to show kindness to others. Therefore, Allahﷻ scolds them.

 أَرَءَيْتَ ٱلَّذِى يُكَذِّبُ بِٱلدِّينِ ۝

Have you seen him who belies the Religion?

فَذَٰلِكَ ٱلَّذِى يَدُعُّ ٱلْيَتِيمَ ٢

That is the one who drives away the orphan,

وَلَا يَحُضُّ عَلَىٰ طَعَامِ ٱلْمِسْكِينِ ٣

and does not urge upon feeding the poor

فَوَيْلٌ لِّلْمُصَلِّينَ ٤

So woe be to those performers of Salat

ٱلَّذِينَ هُمْ عَن صَلَاتِهِمْ سَاهُونَ ٥

those who are themselves unmindful of their Salat

ٱلَّذِينَ هُمْ يُرَآءُونَ ٦

those who are themselves showy

وَيَمْنَعُونَ ٱلْمَاعُونَ ٧

and refrain from acts of kindness

## Look for your chances

A good Muslim should always look for chances to help others. A good Muslim is kind to others. Muslims should help those who have difficulties. We can help others by giving zakat. You can also help your family by doing chores at home. You can be kind to others by saying, "*Jazakallah khair*," or "May Allahﷻ bless you," or "May Allahﷻ protect you." When someone does a good job, say "*Masha-Allah*." Saying nice words with a smile is being kind.

Islam teaches us to be kind to our parents. When they become old, we should still treat them with respect and be kind to them.

We should talk to them politely. Our Nabiﷺ said that Allahﷻ is kind to people who are kind to others. Our Nabiﷺ also said that Allahﷻ loves kind people.

If you are kind to someone, it does not mean you are weak. You can be kind to someone only if you are strong. A **hero** is someone who is brave and kind, not someone who is mean.

Every day we have many chances to be kind. Can you think of new ways to be kind to your friend, brother, sister, mother, and father?

**Words that I learned today:**

Kindness • Praise • Idol worshipper • al-Ma'un
Jazakallah khair • Masha-Allah • Hero

1. Color all the ovals that show the correct meaning of kindness:

Help or support
someone

Not being mean
to others

Give someone
a hard time

Make things
easy for others

2. Write three different ways that you can be kind to your mother or father.

do chores

help them

show respect

3. Write two different ways that you can be kind to your friend.

help them

show respect.

4. Write T if the sentence is true. Write F if the sentence is false.

We have to be kind only to our parents, not to others. ___F___

We have to be kind only to people, not to animals. ___F___

Allah﷾ is kind to people who are kind to others. ___T___

5. Mark with a ✓ if it is an act of kindness. Mark with an ✗ if it is rude or mean.

I feed hungry birds or cats. ✓

I smile at my friends. ✓

I knock my friend's books onto the floor. ✗

I water the plants in my garden. ✓

I push others while standing in the lunch line. ✗

# Respect

Assalamu alaikum. Welcome to the class. Let us color these two boys who are **greeting** each other with respect.

## Respect

**Respect** means treating someone or something with honor. Respect also means being polite to others. Giving attention to someone is another form of respect. For example, the teacher wants students to pay attention in class. When students pay attention, they show respect. People around us also want our attention. When we give them our attention, we show them respect.

## Golden Rule

Respect is something that everybody wants. You might have heard about the **Golden Rule** of behavior. This rule teaches us that we should treat others the way we want to be treated. Do you want someone to be mean to you? If not, then you should not be mean to others. We should show respect to everyone.

## Respect for others

So far, we have learned that respect is about how we treat others. Our parents love us very much and we love our parents. Allah﷾ tells us to respect our parents. Good Muslims never treat their parents badly. We should never say any bad words to them. Being polite to them and paying attention to them is showing them respect.

## Respect for our Nabi ﷺ

Nabi Muhammad ﷺ is the last messenger for the whole world. We love him and respect him. When we say his name, we add "**Sallahu Alaihi Wa Sallam**" to show respect. In this book, we use the following Arabic word after our Nabi's name to show that we respect him.

### Sallahu Alaihi Wa Sallam

Allah ﷻ sent many nabis and rasuls before Muhammad ﷺ. We must respect all the nabis and rasuls in the same way. After all the other nabis and rasuls' names, we say "**Alaihi Sallam**". This means "peace be upon him."

After Allah's name, we say, "**Subhan-hu wa Ta'ala**" to show respect. The Qur'an is the Book of Allah ﷻ. We touch it with clean hands, and we should keep it clean. We respect the Qur'an and take care of it. We read the Qur'an with respect.

After Allah's name we say: *Subhan-hu wa ta'ala*

After Nabi Muhammad's name, we say: *Sallahu Alahi wa Sallam*

After any other nabi's name, we say: *Alahi sallam*

## Respect for property

Respect is not just about how we behave with others. Respect is also about how we treat the **property** of others. Property or belongings can be toys, books, bikes, cars or even a house. We cannot take or borrow other people's property without asking their permission. We should not harm other people's property.

As Muslims, we should not make fun of other religions, even though Islam is the only religion of Allah. Even today, some people worship pictures and idols, thinking these are their gods. We should not make fun of them. They worship these objects because it is their faith.

## Do not laugh at others

We show respect to others by being nice to them. If someone is nice to us, we should be nicer. Allah teaches us not to laugh at others because they may be better than us. The Qur'an teaches us not to **tease**, or make fun of others. It is not nice to call other people names.

## When someone is away

We show respect when we are with a person. We also show respect when we are not with him or her. We do not speak badly about a person when he or she is away from us. Allah does not like it and He warns us not to do such things.

## Respect privacy

The Qur'an teaches us to respect the **privacy** of other people. Privacy means what you do not want others to see or know. We should not try to find out what others are doing in their own home and on their own time. The Qur'an teaches us to enter people's homes after getting permission. This is to show respect for them. When someone is talking, we should listen carefully. We should speak only when he or she is done speaking.

We should show respect to everything and everyone around us. This makes the world a better place to live.

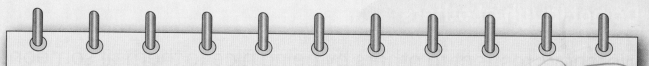

We need not show respect for other religions.     True / ~~False~~

We need not show respect for poor people.     True / False

We touch the Qur'an with _____ to show respect.

**Words that I learned today:**
Greeting • Respect • Golden Rule • Property
Tease • Privacy

1. What is respect?

_Showing kindness_

2. How should a good Muslim treat his or her mother?

_with respect_

3. Color the correct box. We must show respect for:

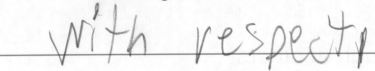

| All the messengers | Muhammad ﷺ only | None of the messengers |

4. Color the correct box. We must show respect for:

| Islam only | All religions | None of the religions |

5. If someone says, "Assalamu alaikum," what should we say in return?

_Wa alaikum_

6. Circle all the correct answers. As a good Muslim, I show respect to a:

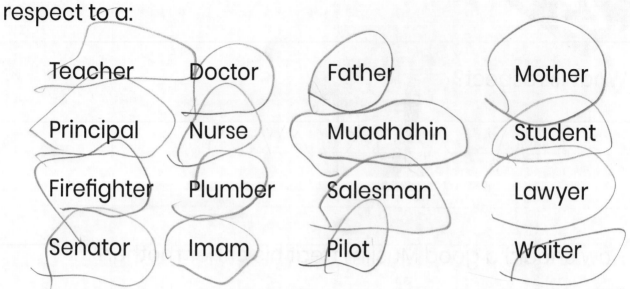

Teacher    Doctor    Father    Mother

Principal    Nurse    Muadhdhin    Student

Firefighter    Plumber    Salesman    Lawyer

Senator    Imam    Pilot    Waiter

7. Why should we not laugh at others?

it is not kind

# Responsibility

Assalamu alaikum. Welcome to the class. Let us color this girl, who is a safe bicycle rider. She is responsible, wears a helmet, and rides her bike carefully.

## Responsibility

**Responsibility** is a long word. It means doing something that is a duty or a job. The person responsible for a duty or job does it because it is required of him or her.

If your teacher tells you to do your homework, then you are responsible for completing it on time. Your homework is your duty, so you are responsible for doing it.

## Failure of duty

If a person fails to complete his or her duty, then the person is **irresponsible**. The person does not respect the importance of the duty. He or she is careless and cannot be trusted. An irresponsible person can put himself or herself in danger, or put others in danger.

Your bus driver is responsible for safely picking you up in the morning and dropping you off after school. The driver is responsible for dropping you off on the right street, at the right time, and at the right place. Imagine what might happen if the driver drops you off on the wrong street or at the wrong time.

## Responsibility with age

We are responsible for something that we own or **control**. As a child, you are not responsible for driving a car. If you have a bike, then you are responsible for riding it safely. If you have a pet, then you have to feed it and take care of it. As you grow up, your responsibilities will increase.

## Use your brain

Responsibility also means to think, use our brain, and act in a smart way. If you turn off a running water **faucet**, then you acted responsibly. Nobody had to tell you to turn off the faucet. You knew that it was wrong to let the water run. The person who left the faucet running was irresponsible. You were responsible because you understood the value of acting properly.

If somebody tells you to do something bad, you should think twice. If you decide not to do it, then you have acted responsibly.

## A good Muslim

Islam teaches us to be responsible people. A good Muslim respects his or her duties. A good Muslim finishes his or her work on time. Allahﷻ requires us to do salat at specific times. We can learn to be responsible by praying on time. A responsible person uses his or her time wisely.

During Ramadan, we learn responsibility. We learn to control our hunger. We are responsible for our own salat and our own fasting. Nobody else can do our salat or fasting for us. We pay zakat to needy people. Giving zakat is our responsibility. During Hajj, we perform many duties. These duties should be performed on the right day of the right month. If we fail to do these duties, then Hajj becomes invalid.

## Responsibility in masjid

While in a masjid, we can practice being responsible. We learn to sit quietly while the Imam is talking. We are responsible for keeping our shoes in the proper place. We respect others and act in a respectful manner.

## Responsibility at home

At home, we are responsible for keeping our bedrooms clean. We should also keep our desk or table clean. We should keep our books in the right place. Once we are done playing, we should put away our toys in the right places. These are our responsibilities. Helping our parents with different **chores** teaches us responsibility.

## No excuses

We should not make **excuses** if we do not finish a task. We are responsible for doing our own tasks. If we leave a job half-way done, then we did not show responsibility. When our parents give us a job to do, we should finish it. We should not have to be reminded again and again.

Blaming others is not good behavior. If we do something wrong, then we should take the blame. Blaming others means walking away from responsibility. This means we are not being truthful.

## Learn responsibility

We cannot learn responsibility in only one day. If we keep trying every day, we will become responsible. It is up to you to become a responsible person. Nobody likes an irresponsible person. Everybody loves a responsible person. Allahﷻ loves people who are responsible.

**Words that I learned today:**
Responsibility • Irresponsible • Control
Faucet • Chores • Excuses

1. What is responsibility?

_____

_____

2. Write four things that you are responsible for doing. (Think of anything that you own or control.)

A. _____

B. _____

C. _____

D. _____

3. As a responsible person, what should you do when you hear the adhan?

_____

4. As a responsible person, what should you do when the Imam is talking?

_____

5. Will your responsibilities increase as you grow older?

Write Yes or No. _____

6. Are you a responsible child? Some tasks for you are listed below. For each task, color the answer that applies to you.

A. After dinner,

| I put my plate in the sink. | I leave my plate on the table. | I ask my mom to take my plate. |

B. When my clothes are dirty, I put them

in the laundry basket.    on the floor.    with my clean clothes.

C. After I finish playing a video game,

| I leave the game on the floor. | my dad cleans up my mess. | I put the game away. |

# Obedience

Assalamu alaikum. Welcome to the class. Let us color this boy who obeys Allah﷾, and has just completed his salat.

## Obedience

**Obedience** means to follow the orders of an elder or someone who has **authority**. An authority is someone who has the power and the right to give an order. For example, an authority can be a leader, a governor, an imam, or the president. For Muslims, our ultimate authority is Allah﷾ and His Rasulﷺ. We show obedience to them. This means we **obey** their orders.

## Obedience to Allah﷾

Allah﷾ ordered us to do salat five times a day. He told us to be truthful and kind. He also required us to follow the teachings in the Qur'an. If we listen to Allah's﷾ orders, then we are **obedient** to Him. If we do not obey Allah﷾, then we are not good Muslims.

Allah﷾ also asked us to obey Rasulullahﷺ. Allah﷾ sent Nabi Muhammadﷺ to show us how to live and how to treat others. If we obey Rasulullahﷺ, then we are obeying Allah﷾.

## Obedience to parents

Allah﷾ told us to listen to our parents. The Qur'an says that obedience to Allah﷾ comes first. Obedience and kindness to parents comes second. We should always obey our parents, because they want the best for us. They never stop loving us. For their love and kindness, we have to be kind and obedient to them in return.

First, we obey: _____Allah_____

Second, we obey our: _____parents_____

## How to obey parents

How do we obey our parents? We do not say "no" to them. When our parents tell us to study, it is for our **benefit**. When they call us for salat, it is for our benefit. When they tell us to go to bed, it is for our benefit. We should not argue with them. We should not refuse to help them or make excuses.

## Obedience to teachers

We should also be good to our teachers. When we are in school, we should obey our teachers. If we do not listen to our teachers, then we cannot learn. The school has rules, so we can learn in a safe place. We have to obey our teachers for our own benefit.

Sometimes you might be with older people, such as uncles, aunts, or grandparents. May be you have older brothers or sisters. You should listen to the people who are older than you.

## Examples of types of obedience

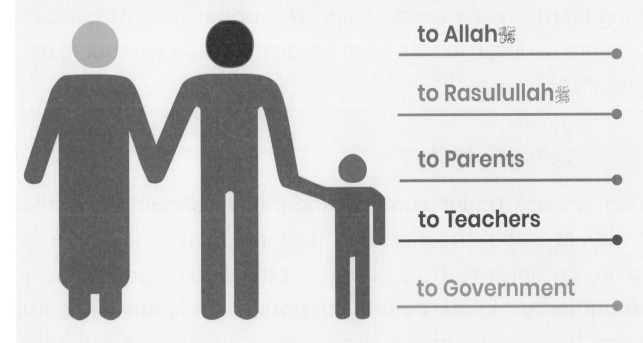

to Allah ﷻ

to Rasulullah ﷺ

to Parents

**to Teachers**

to Government

### To the government

We also show obedience to the laws of our city, state, and country. Our **government** makes the laws. These laws are made for a reason—to try to run the country properly.

### Do not obey Shaitan

We should not obey Shaitan. He acts as if he is our friend, but he is really our enemy. He tries to make us believe that bad things are good for us. If we obey him, then we will get into trouble. Shaitan does not want good things for us. He is not our friend or teacher. We should never obey Shaitan.

If you do not know someone, you have to be careful about obeying them. An **unknown** person, a stranger, may be good or bad. Before we listen to someone we do not know, we should ask our parents.

## Obedience to authority

When we are under some authority, we should obey the authority. At school, teachers and the principal are the authority. At home, parents are the authority. At the workplace, the boss is the authority. In our country, the president is the authority. Above all these authorities is Allah﷾. He is the highest authority.

We should obey our parents, teachers, and elders. If they tell us not to follow Allah﷾, then we do not need to obey them. This is because obedience to Allah﷾ always comes first. However, we should still be kind to our parents.

Who should we never obey? _Shaitan_

When do we not have to obey our parents? _when they don't say_

**Words that I learned today:**
Obedience • Authority • Obey • Obedient
Benefit • Government • Unknown

1. If we do not obey Allah, can we still be Muslims? Circle Yes or No.

YES          (NO)

2. Write three things that Allah has told us to do.

| | | |
|---|---|---|
| Pray | obey rasul | listen to Parent ts |

3. What does obedience mean?

_____ listen _____

4. Write three ways that you were obedient to your parents this week.

A. _____ studying _____

B. _____ listening _____

C. _____ doing chores _____

5. A. Who pretends to be our friend but is not a real friend?

_____ sheitan _____

B. Should we obey him? Write Yes or No. _____ no _____

6. Circle all the correct answers. As a good Muslim, I obey:

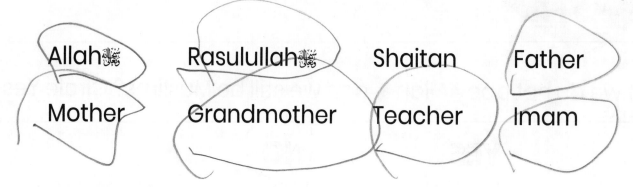

Allah ﷻ   Rasulullah ﷺ   Shaitan   Father

Mother   Grandmother   Teacher   Imam

7. Fill in the blanks using the correct words from the box below.

> learn   Shaitan   benefit   unknown

Salat is for our _____benefit_____.

We do not obey _____Shaitan_____.

I am careful around an _____unknown_____ person.

When we obey the teacher, we _____learn_____ better.

# Cleanliness

Assalamu alaikum. Welcome to the class. Let us begin by coloring Jamilah's bedroom. She keeps her room clean to make her salat.

## Cleanliness

**Cleanliness** means to remain or be kept clean. When we speak of cleanliness, we mean to be free from dirt and germs. We also mean cleaning ourselves by washing our hands or bodies. We also mean cleaning our bodies in the proper Islamic manner.

## Physical cleanliness

Physical cleanliness means cleanliness of our bodies. This is the most important kind. We do not want to be dirty. Every day we do many things that make us dirty. Many household chores make us dirty. Sometimes, not doing anything at all can make us dirty. For example, if we stay outside on a hot day for too long, our bodies sweat. There is also dirt in the air. So, we become dirty.

The easiest way to clean ourselves is to wash our hands, face, and feet. Sometimes, we become so dirty that we need to take a shower.

Cleanliness is part of our worship. We cannot do salat without doing wudu. Every day, we do wudu before our salat. Doing five salat a day means we do wudu five times to clean ourselves. Even if we have taken a shower in the morning, we still must do wudu before salat.

Cleanliness is part of good **hygiene**. Good hygiene means practicing cleanliness so that we do not fall sick. Before eating, we wash our hands. We should brush our teeth at least twice daily—after we wake up in the morning and before going to bed.

We should also wear clean clothes. Clean clothes make us feel good. We need clean clothes to do salat. When we use the bathroom, we should make sure to keep our clothes clean. If our clothes become dirty, we have to change them.

## Mental cleanliness

**Mental** means our minds. The cleanliness of our mind is also important. Cleaning our mind means not allowing bad thoughts or ideas to stay in our minds. A robber thinks about how to rob a person. A bad person thinks about how to hurt another person. We are not robbers or bad people. But sometimes we have bad ideas. When we do, we should say:

أَعُوذُ بِاللَّهِ مِنَ الشَّيْطَانِ الرَّجِيمِ

**Audhu billahi minas shaitanir rajim.**

It means: **I seek Allah's protection from the bad Shaitan**.

We cannot see Shaitan because he is invisible. He whispers bad thoughts. He pretends that he is our friend. He causes us to think bad ideas. For this reason, we seek Allah's protection from the whispering of the bad Shaitan. Before salat, we should make sure our mind is clean.

## Surrounding cleanliness

Physical and mental cleanliness is about your body and mind. But what about your surroundings—the place all around you? Just as clean clothes and a clean body makes us feel good, clean surroundings also makes us feel good. Clean surroundings is also a part of having good hygiene.

No one wants to be in a stinky, bad place. Islam teaches us that we should keep our surroundings clean.

Salat should be done in a clean place. Our salat mat should be clean. When it is time for salat, we use clean mats to pray. We keep our masjid clean. We keep our shoes in the shoe rack in the masjid.

## Clean environment

We also try to keep our environment clean. We should not litter. Our parents are responsible for keeping the environment free from **pollution**. We need clean air to breathe. We need clean water to drink.

## Self-check

Are you a clean person? Let us find out from the following questions. Put a check mark ☑ in the box that applies to you.

|  | Always | Sometimes | Never |
|---|---|---|---|
| I wash my hands before eating. | ☐ | ☐ | ☐ |
| I brush my teeth every day. | ☐ | ☐ | ☐ |
| I keep my bedroom clean. | ☐ | ☐ | ☐ |
| I pray in a clean place. | ☐ | ☐ | ☐ |
| I do wudu without making a mess. | ☐ | ☐ | ☐ |
| I wear clean clothes. | ☐ | ☐ | ☐ |

**Words that I learned today:**

Chores • Hygiene • Mental • Invisible
Whisper • Environment

1. What should we do before salah?

_____

2. Circle the correct answer. Can we make salat when we are dirty?

YES                NO

3. Circle the things that should be clean before we make salat.

Our body        Our clothes    Prayer Rug      Bookshelf

Kitchen         Our mind       Playground      Masjid

4. Circle the places that people should try to keep clean.

Bedroom        Masjid         Classroom       Playground

Living room    Kitchen        Bathroom        Backyard

Dining table   Roads          Hospital        Garden

Garage         Driveway       Neighborhood    Closet

## 5. Solve the crossword puzzle below:

**Across**

1. This is the room where we sleep. We keep it clean.

2. Something that covers our feet.

3. We follow Islam, so this is our identity.

**Down**

4. We take a shower to make us this.

5.  Opposite of clean.

6.  We keep our shoes in the _____ in the masjid.

7. This is the place where we go for salat. We keep these places clean.

# Honesty

Assalamu alaikum. Welcome to the class. Let us color the daughter telling her mom that she broke a toy.

## Honesty

In Lesson 23, we learned about truthfulness. Truthfulness means that we speak the truth. We should tell the truth, so other people will trust us.

Today, we are going to learn about **honesty**. Honesty means to behave in a truthful and sincere manner. An honest person does not cheat, steal, or tell a lie. Truthfulness is about speaking the truth and honesty is about behaving in a sincere manner. We can show honesty in two ways:

1. What we say
2. What we do

## Honesty to everything

An honest person is honest to everyone. The person is even honest with himself or herself. Even if no one is watching, an honest person does the right thing. An honest person knows that even if no one is watching, Allah﷾ is watching.

An honest person always speaks and behaves truthfully. An honest person does not cheat others. Allah﷾ told us that some people cheat others by giving them less than they deserve. The cheater collects the full price for an item, but gives the buyer less in quantity or quality. The cheater thinks that he or she will becoming rich. Allahﷻ says these cheaters will suffer severe punishment.

## Story time

Let us read the following story, and consider what we would do.

*Your father left his glass of juice on the table. You were jumping around and hit the glass. The juice spilled onto the prayer rug. When your father returned, he thought the cat probably tipped over the glass. The cat cannot say that you spilled the juice. What should you do? Should you say you are sorry, and tell your father that it was not the cat?*

Honesty also means that we keep our word. When we say we will or will not do something, we should keep our word. Here is another story:

*You have a nice, new game that you like very much. You shared it with your friend. At first, he said he would give it back to you. But now he does not want to give it back. He is not keeping his word. How would you feel?*

## Nabi Muhammadﷺ

When people are honest, we know we can trust them. Nabi Muhammadﷺ was known as **Al-Amin**, the **trustworthy** one.

People trusted him because he never lied. We should learn from the example of our Nabiﷺ.

The life of Nabi Muhammadﷺ shows us that honesty is an important part of being a Muslim. He showed us that we have to be honest and sincere all the time. We should be honest in our worship, our behavior, our words—everything we do. We should not cheat, falsify, mislead, or misinform others.

Nabi Muhammadﷺ said, "Truthfulness leads to righteousness, and righteousness leads to Paradise. In addition, a man keeps on telling the truth until he becomes a truthful person. Falsehood leads to wickedness and evil-doing, and wickedness leads to the [Hell] Fire, and a man may keep on telling lies, till he is written before God as a liar."

## More story time

*Your neighbor asked you to pull weeds in his yard. He said he would give you a nickel for each weed. After you pulled many weeds, he did not want to give you the money. Was this man being honest? Would you pull weeds for him again?*

Honesty also means that we respect the homes and property of others. If something does not belong to us, we cannot take it secretly. This is stealing. Some property belongs to the local government. We should not damage such property.

*You were riding your scooter, and then you went inside for Asr salah. When you went back outside, your scooter was gone. Somebody did not respect your property—your scooter. This person was not honest. We should not take other people's property unless they give it to us.*

Honesty means we do not cheat, even when nobody is looking. We should remember that Allahﷻ is always watching us.

*You were playing a board game with a friend. You were winning the game. You left the room to get some cookies. When you returned, it looked like your friend changed the dice. He was not honest; he cheated. He won the game. How would you feel? Would you play another game with this friend?*

Allahﷻ told us to be honest and truthful. We should stand up for the truth. All the nabis and rasuls taught us to be truthful. They always behaved honestly and did what was right, even when it was difficult.

**Words that I learned today:**

Honesty • Al-Amin • Trust • Trustworthy

1. Circle T if the sentence is true. Circle F if the sentence is false.

Honesty means we admit our mistakes.      (T) F

Honesty means we do not cheat.      (T) F

Honesty means we keep our word.      (T) F

Honesty means we do not trust others.      T (F)

Honesty means we take things without asking.      T (F)

2. People always liked to do business with Rasulullahﷺ because he was honest. People gave him a nice name because he was trustworthy. Write the name in the space below?

<u>Mohamad (SAW)</u>

3. Circle Yes if the sentence is correct. Circle No if the sentence is incorrect.

Honesty means behaving only in the mosque.      Yes (No)

We are honest if we tell the truth.      (Yes) No

A Muslim should always try to be honest.      (Yes) No

Allahﷻ loves honest people.      (Yes) No

# Appendix

# Steps of Salāh

## Physical preparation for salāh:

**Physical cleanliness:** Before performing salāh, make sure your body is clean. You must complete *wudu*, and be in the state of *wudu*. During the salāh, do not look sideways, do not look at others, and do not talk to others. Do not make unnecessary movements. Do not scratch, yawn, laugh, or smile. If you must sneeze or cough, that is fine, but try to minimize the noise.

**Clean clothes:** Your clothes should be clean and should cover your body. For boys, clothes should cover the body at least from the navel to the knees. For girls, clothes should cover the body from the neck to the ankles, and to the wrists. The head should be covered, but the face can remain uncovered. Clothes should not be transparent. Avoid any clothing that has pictures of people, animals, or offensive writing.

**Clean place:** You should find a clean place to make your salāh. A prayer rug is not necessary. A prayer rug should always be clean, so it ensures a clean place while you are praying.

**Direction to face:** You should face *Qiblah*, which is the direction of the Ka'bah in Makkah.

**Time:** *Fard* (compulsory) prayers are performed at the proper time. It is preferable to perform the prayer as soon as the *Adhān* (call to prayer) is announced.

**Mental preparation:** We begin the prayer with full mental and physical attention. During salāh, we are worshipping and talking directly to Allāh, therefore, we must provide our total attention. Avoid any place or object that diverts your full attention.

**What is a raka'ah?** Each salāh can be divided into cycles of physical postures, or raka'at. Each raka'ah involves the positions of *qiyam* (standing), *ruku* (bowing), *sujud* (prostration), *jalsa* (sitting), another *sujud* (prostration), and associated recitations. The chart shows the specified number of raka'at for the five daily salāh. Some variation in the number of Sunnah prayers exists among the madhhab.

|  | Sunnah raka'at before Fard raka'at | Fard raka'at | Sunnah raka'at after Fard raka'at |
|---|---|---|---|
| Fajr | 2 | 2 |  |
| Dhuhr | 4 | 4 | 2 |
| 'Asr | 4 | 4 |  |
| Maghrib |  | 3 | 2 |
| 'Isha | 4 | 4 | 2, then 3 (wajib) |

## Description for a salāh of two raka'at:

The following description of steps is for a salāh with two raka'at (for example, the Fard prayer of Fajr). At the end of this description, there are brief notes about how to perform three or four raka'at of salāh.

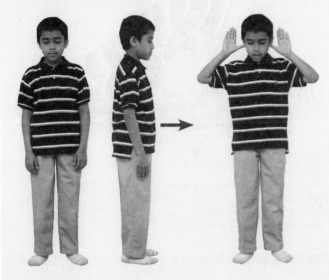

**Step 1** (Figures above)

When you stand up for salāh, make an intention to perform the salāh for the sake of Allāh. Say to yourself (in any language) that you intend to offer this *Salāh* (*Fajr, Dhuhr, Asr, Maghrib,* or *Isha*), *Fard, Sunnat,* or *Witr,* and the number of raka'ahs (example—"I intend to offer two *raka'ah* of *Fard, Fajr* prayer for Allāh").

**Position:** *Qiyam.* Stand upright. Raise both hands up to the ears (palms and body facing the direction of the Ka'bah).

**What to say:** "*Allāhu Akbar.*" (Allāh is the Greatest).

**Step 2** (Figures on the right)

**Position:** Place your left hand over your belly, place your right hand on top of the left hand, and grip the wrist of the left hand.

## What to say:

1. "*Subhanaka Allāhumma wa bihamdika, wa tabārakasmuka, wa ta'āla jadduka, wa lā ilāha ghairuka.*" (This part is known as *thana.* It means "Glory be to you, O Allāh, and praise to You. Blessed be Your Name, exalted be Your Majesty and Glory. There is no god but You.")

2. "*A'ūdu billāhi mina ash-Shaytānir rajim.*" (I seek the protection of Allāh against Shaitān, the condemned.)

3. "*Bismillāhir rahmānir rahīm.*" (In the Name of Allāh, Most Gracious, Most Merciful.)

4. Now recite Sūrah Al-Fātihah. We must recite Sūrah Al-Fātihah during each raka'ah. A salāh is not valid if Sūrah Al-Fātihah is not recited.

"*Al humdu li-llahi rabbi-l 'alamīn. Ar-rahmāni-r rahīm. Māliki yawmi-d dīn. Iyyāka na'budu wa iyyāka Nāsta'īn. Ihdina-s sirāta-l mustaqīm. Sirātal ladhīna an'amta 'alaihim, ghairil maghdūbi 'alaihim, wa la-d dāllīn. (Āmīn.)*"

(The Praise belongs to Allāh, The Rabb of all the worlds; the Rahman; the Rahim. Malik of the Day of Judgment. You alone do we serve, and to You alone we seek help. Guide us on the Right Path—the path of those upon whom You have bestowed favors; not of those upon whom wrath is brought down, nor those gone astray.)

5. After reciting sūrah Fātihah, we now recite any short sūrah or a few verses from the Qur'ān. This additional recitation of part of the Qur'ān is done during the first two raka'ah only. It is always good to memorize as many sūrah as you can, so you can recite them during your salāh.

## Step 3

(Figures above)

**What to say:** "*Allāhu Akbar.*"

**Position:** This position is called *ruku*. Bow with your back perpendicular to your legs. Place your hands on your knees. Do not bend the knees.

**What to say:** "*Subhana rabbiyal 'Adhīm.*" Say this three times. (Glorified is my Rabb, the Great.)

## Step 4

(Figures below)

While going back to the *qiyam* (upright) position,

**What to say:** "*Samia Allāhu liman hamidah.*" (Allāh listens to him who praises Him.)

**Position**: In *qiyam* position.

**What to say:** "*Rabbanā wa laka al hamd.*" (Our Rabb, praise be for You only.)

## Step 5

(Figure above)

**What to say:** While moving to the next position of *sujud*, say "*Allāhu Akbar.*"

**Position:** This position is *sujud*. Place both of your knees on the floor. Try not to move the position of your feet, that is, do not move your feet away from the *qiyam* position. After placing the knees, place your two hands on the floor with palms touching the floor. Do not glide your hands on the floor. Your elbow is not on the floor. Your hands should be sufficiently apart to leave room for your head. Now place your forehead on the floor. Both your nose and forehead should touch the floor. Your hands are on the side of your head. Your stomach will not touch the floor. You should be the most humble in this position.

The most powerful part of our body is our brain, the site of our intelligence. We submit our full selves, with full understanding, to Almighty Allāh. We realize that our strength, power, wealth, and everything that we have is from Allāh. To emphasize this physical and spiritual humility, we will repeat the *sujud* position again in Step 7.

**What to say:** "*Subhana rabbiyal A'ala.*" (Say this three times. Glory be to Allāh, the Exalted.)

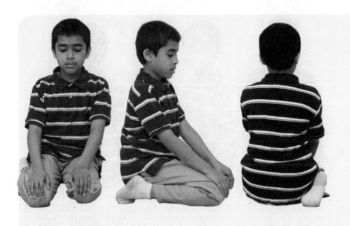

### Step 6 (Figures above)

The next position is *jalsa*.

**What to say:** While moving to the *jalsa* position, say *"Allāhu Akbar."*

**Position:** To move to *jalsa* position, rise from *sujud*. First you will raise your head off the floor, then you will raise your hands. Now you are sitting on the floor— this posture is called *jalsa*.

**What to say:** *"Rabbi-ghfir lī wa rhamnī."* (O my Rabb, forgive me and have mercy on me.)

### Step 7 (Figure above)

We will repeat *sujud* again. Every *raka'ah* has two *sujud*.

**What to say:** While moving to the sujud position, say *"Allāhu Akbar."*

**Position:** *Sujud*. Place your palms on the floor and then your forehead. Both the nose and the forehead should be touching the floor.

**What to say:** *"Subhāna rabbiyal A'ala."* Say this three times. (Glory to Allāh, the Exalted.)

**This completes one raka'ah.**

### Step 8 (Figures above)

Rise to the *qiyam* (standing) position. The movement should be in a systematic, graceful manner. First you will raise your forehead from the floor, next you will raise your hands and then you will raise your knees. Try not to move your feet—that is, the position of your feet should be the same as it was during the first raka'ah.

**What to say:** While moving to the qiyam position, say *"Allāhu Akbar."*

**Position:** Stand upright. Hold the left hand with the right hand on top.

**What to say:** Sūrah Al-Fātihah, then any short sūrah or a few verses from the Qur'ān.

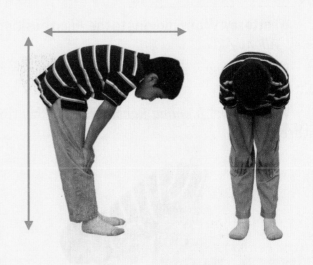

## Step 9

(Figures on the previous page)

**What to say:** *"Allāhu Akbar."*

**Position:** *Ruku.* Bow with your back perpendicular to your legs. Place your hands on your knees.

**What to say:** *"Subhāna rabbiyal 'Adhīm."* Say this three times.

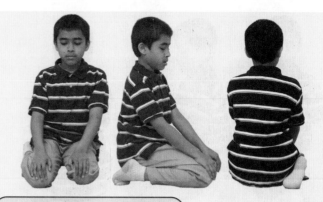

## Step 12

(Figures above)

**What to say:** While moving to the jalsa position, say *"Allāhu Akbar."*

**Position:** Rise from the *sujud* position. Now you are sitting in the *jalsa* position.

**What to say:** *"Rabbi-ghfir lī wa rhamnī"* (O my Rabb, forgive me and have Mercy on me.)

## Step 10

(Figures above)

**Position:** While moving back to the *qiyam* (standing) position,

**What to say:** *"Sami'a Allāhu liman hamidah."*

**Position:** In *qiyam* position. You are upright.

**What to say:** *"Rabbanā wa lakal hamd."*

## Step 11

(Figure below)

**What to say:** While moving to the sujud position, say *"Allāhu Akbar."*

**Position:** *Sujud.* Follow the same sequence as in Step 5.

**What to say:** *"Subhāna Rabbiyal A'ala."* Say this three times.

## Step 13

(Figure above)

**What to say:** While moving to the sujud position, say *"Allāhu Akbar."*

**Position:** *Sujud.* First place your hands and then your forehead on the floor.

**What to say:** *"Subhāna Rabbiyal A'ala."* Say this three times.

## Step 14

(Figures in the next page)

**What to say:** While going to the jalsa position, say *"Allāhu Akbar."*

**Position:** Rise from the *sujud* position. Now you are sitting in the *jalsa* position.

**What to say:** Say *Tashahud, Durūd,* and a short prayer as follows:

*"At-tahiyātu lillahi was-salawātu wattaiyibātu. Assalāmu 'alayka ayyuhan-nabiyu wa rahmat-ullāhi wa barakātuhu. Assalāmu 'alainā wa 'ala 'ibadi-llāhis-sālihīn. Ashhadu an lā ilāha illallāhu wa ashhadu anna Muhammadan 'abduhu wa rasūluhu."*

(All these salutations, prayers, and nice comments are for Allāh. Peace be on you, O Nabi, and the blessings of Allāh, and His grace. Peace on us and on all the righteous servants of Allāh. I bear witness that none but Allāh is worthy of worship, and I bear witness that Muhammad is the servant and messenger of Allāh.) This is known as *Tashahud.*

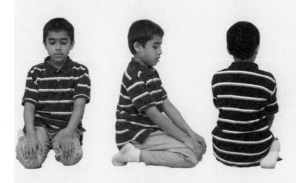

**Position:** Raise your right index finger, so it is pointing upward, while reciting the last part of this prayer.

Next you will recite the *Durūd.*

*"Allāhumma salli 'ala Muhammadin wa 'ala āli Muhummadin, kamā sallayta 'ala Ibrāhima, wa ala āli Ibrāhima, innaka hamidun majid. Allāhumma barik 'ala Muhammadin wa 'ala āli Muhummadin, kama barakta ala Ibrāhima, wa 'ala āli Ibrahīm, innaka hamīdun majīd."*

(O Allāh, send your Mercy on Muhammad and his posterity as you sent Your mercy on Ibrāhīm and his posterity. You are the Most Praised, The Most Glorious. O Allāh, send your Blessings on Muhammad and his posterity as you have blessed Ibrāhīm and his posterity. You are the Most praised, The Most Glorious.)

Now you may add a short prayer, such as:

*"Rabbanā ātinā fi-d dunyā hasanatan wa fi-l ākhirati hasanatan, wa qinā 'adhāban nār."*

(Our Rabb, give us the good of this world, and good in the Hereafter, and save us from the chastisement of Fire.)

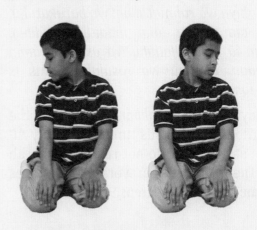

**Step 15** (Figure above left)

**Position:** Slowly turn your head and face right. This is called *salam.*

**What to say:** *"As-salāmu 'alaikum wa rahma-tullāh."* (Peace and mercy of Allāh be on you.)

**Step 16** (Figure above right)

**Position:** Slowly turn your head and face left. This is called *salam.*

**What to say:** *"As-salāmu 'alaikum wa rahma-tullāh."*

**This completes the two raka'at of salāh.**

## How to pray three raka'at (Maghrib)

In order to perform a three-raka'at salah, use all the postures and prayers up to step 13.

In step 14, recite up to *"At-tahiyātu lillahi was-salawātu wattaiyibātu. Assalāmu 'alayka ayyuhan-nabiyu wa rahmatullāhi wa barakātuhu. Assalāmu 'alainā wa 'ala 'ibadi-llāhis-sālihīn. Ashhadu an lā ilāha illallāhu wa ashhadu anna Muhammadan 'abduhu wa rasūluhu."* This is known as *Tashahud*.

After saying *"Allāhu akbar,"* return to the *qiyam* position, step 8. This time recite only *Al-Fātihah* (in step 8), but do not recite any sūrah or part of the Qur'ān. All prayers and postures are the same as shown in steps 9–16.

## How to pray four raka'at

## (Dhuhr, 'Asr, and 'Isha)

In order to perform a four-raka'at salāh, use all the postures and prayers up to step 13.

In Step 14, only the *Tashahud* prayer will be recited, and the *qiyam* position, in step 8, will be resumed.

In step 8, only *Al-Fātihah* will be recited without adding any sūrah. Steps 8–13 complete the third raka'ah. The *qiyam* position in step 8 will be resumed.

In step 8, only *Al-Fātihah* will be recited without adding any sūrah. Steps 8–16, complete the fourth raka'ah.

### From the Qur'an

...keep up the salāt, as salāt controls indecent and unacceptable behaviors... *(Sūrah Al-'Ankabūt, 29:45)*

Take care to do your salāt, praying in the best way, and stand before Allāh with full devotion. *(Sūrah Al-Baqarah, 2:238)*

# Outline of Curriculum – Levels 1, 2 and 3

Each year the curriculum begins with a few topics on Allāh, the Qur'ān, the Nabi, the Hadīth, or Sunnah. In the early years, emphasis is placed on the five-pillars, and each year, this emphasis increases. Every year, a history of some of the messengers is introduced in an age-appropriate manner. Several lessons are devoted to Islamic manners, values, and morals so that children grow up with a good understanding of Islamic culture. Each lesson includes a short homework assignment.

| Level 1 | Level 2 | Level 3 |
|---|---|---|
| **Unit 1: Aqaid: Our Belief** | **Unit 1: The Creator–His Message** | **Unit 1: Knowing About Allah** |
| Allāh: Our Creator | Allāh: Our Creator | Who is Allāh? |
| Islam | How Does Allāh Create? | What Allāh Is and Is Not |
| Our Faith | Allāh: What Does He Do? | Allāh: The Most-Merciful |
| Nabi Muhammad | What Does Allāh Not Do | Allāh: The Best Judge |
| The Qur'an | The Qur'an | What Does Allāh Want Us to Do? |
| **Unit 2: Knowing Allāh** | Hadith and Sunnah | **Unit 2: Teachings of Islam** |
| Allāh Loves Us | **Unit 2: Our Ibadat** | We Are Muslims: We Have 'Iman |
| Remembering Allāh | Shahadah: The First Pillar | Belief in the Qur'an |
| Allāh Rewards Us | Salah: The Second Pillar | Belief in the Messengers |
| **Unit 3: Our Ibadat** | Zakah: The Third Pillar | Hadīth and Sunnah |
| Five Pillars of Islam | Sawm: The Fourth Pillar | Jinn |
| Shahadah: The First Pillar | Hajj: The Fifth Pillar | Muslims in North America |
| Salah: The Second Pillar | Wudu: Keeping Our Bodies Clean | The Straight Path: The Right Path |
| Zakat: The Third Pillar | **Unit 3: Messengers of Allah** | **Unit 3: Life of Nabi Muhammad** |
| Fasting: The Fourth Pillar | Ibrahim (A): A Friend of Allah | Kindness of Rasūlullāh |
| Hajj: The Fifth Pillar | Yaqub (A) and Yusuf (A) | How Rasūlullāh Treated Others |
| **Unit 4: Messengers of Allah** | Musa (A) and Harun (A) | Our Relationship with Rasūlullāh |
| Adam (A): The First Nabi | Yunus (A) | **Unit 4: Messengers of Allah** |
| Nuh (A): Saved From Flood | Muhammad: Rasulullah | Ismā'īl (A) and Ishāq (A) |
| Ibrahim (A): Never Listen to Shaitan | **Unit 4: Learning About Islam** | Shua'ib (A): A Nabi of Allāh |
| Musa (A): Challenging A Bad Ruler | Obey Allāh, Obey Rasul | Dāwūd (A): A Nabi of Allāh |
| Isa (A): A Great Nabi of Allāh | Day of Judgment and the Hereafter | 'Isā (A): A Nabi of Allāh |
| **Unit 5: Other Basics of Islam** | Our Masjid | **Unit 5: Learning About Islam** |
| Angels: They Always Work for Allāh | Common Islamic Phrases | Ka'bah |
| Shaitan: Our Enemy | Food that We May Eat | Masjid Nabawī |
| Makkah and Madinah | **Unit 5: Akhlaq and Adab in Islam** | Bilāl ibn Rabāh |
| Eid: Two Festivals | Truthfulness | Zaid ibn Hārithah |
| **Unit 6: Akhlaq and Adab in Islam** | Kindness | **Unit 6: Akhlaq and Adab in Islam** |
| Good Manners | Respect | Being Kind: A Virtue of the Believers |
| Kindness and Sharing | Responsibility | Forgiveness: A Good Quality |
| Respect | Obedience | Good Deeds: A Duty of the Believers |
| Forgiveness | Cleanliness | Perseverance: Never Give Up |
| Thanking Allāh | Honesty | Punctuality: Doing Things on Time |

# Outline of Curriculum – Levels 4, 5 and 6

By Level 5, students have learned the biography of the Nabi Muhammad☙, including a summary of the events that shaped his life and early Islam. By Level 6, students will have read the biographies of most of the prominent messengers. At this stage, students will have learned all the fundamental principles and key concepts of Islam. Even if students do not attend weekend schools after Level 6, they have already gained significant knowledge about Islam.

| Level 4 | Level 5 | Level 6 |
|---|---|---|
| **Unit 1: Knowing the Creator** | **Unit 1: The Creator, His Message** | **Unit 1: The Creator–His Message** |
| Rewards of Allāh☙: Everybody Receives Them | Tawhīd, Kāfir, Kufr, Shirk, Nifāq | Attributes of Allāh☙ |
| Discipline of Allāh☙ | Why Should We Worship Allāh☙? | The Promise of Allāh☙ |
| Names of Allāh☙ | Revelation of the Qur'ān | **Unit 2: The Qur'ān and Hadith** |
| Books of Allāh☙ | Characteristics of the Messengers | Objective of the Qur'an? |
| **Unit 2: How Islam Changed Arabia** | **Unit 2: The Battles, Developments** | Compilation of the Qur'ān |
| Pre-Islamic Arabia | Pledges of 'Aqabah | Previous Books and the Qur'ān |
| The Year of the Elephant | The Battle of Badr | Compilation of Hadīth |
| Early Life of Muhammad☙ | The Battle of Uhud | **Unit 3: Fundamentals of Deen** |
| Life Before Becoming a Nabi | The Battle of the Trench | The Importance of Shahādah |
| First Revelation | The Treaty of Hudaibiyah | Khushū in Salāt |
| Makkah Period | Liberation of Makkah | Taqwā: A Quality of Believers |
| Hijrat to Madīnah | **Unit 3: The Messengers of Allāh** | **Unit 4: Messengers of Allāh** |
| Madīnah Period | Adam (A): The Creation of Mankind | Nūh (A) |
| **Unit 3: The Rightly Guided Khalīfah** | Ibrāhīm (A) Debate with Polytheists | Tālūt, Jālūt, and Dāwūd (A) |
| Abū Bakr: The First Khalifah | Ibrāhīm (A): Plan Against Idols | Dāwūd (A) and Sulaimān (A) |
| 'Umar ibn al-Khattāb | Luqmān (A): A Wise Man's Lifelong Teachings | Mūsā (A) and Fir'awn |
| 'Uthmān ibn 'Affān | Yūsuf (A): His Childhood | Mūsā (A) and Khidir |
| 'Ali ibn Abū Tālib | Yūsuf (A): His Righteousness | 'Isā (A) and Maryam (ra) |
| **Unit 4: The Messengers of Allāh** | Yūsuf (A): Dream Comes True | **Unit 5: Prominent Muslimahs** |
| Hūd (A): Struggle to Guide People | Ayyūb (A): Patience, Perseverance | Khadījah (ra) |
| Sālih (A): To Guide the Misguided | Zakariyyāh (A), Yahyā (A) | 'A'ishah (ra) |
| Mūsā (A): His Life and Actions | **Unit 4: Islam in the World** | Fātimah (ra) |
| Sulaimān (A): A Humble King | Major Masājid in the World | Some Prominent Muslimahs |
| **Unit 5: Fiqh of Salāt** | **Unit 5: Islamic Values, Teachings** | **Unit 6: Knowledge Enrichment** |
| Preparation for Salāt | Upholding Truth: A Duty for All Believers | Al-Qiyāmah: The Awakening |
| Requirements of Salāt | Responsibility and Punctuality | Rūh and Nafs |
| Mubtilāt us-Salāt | My Mind My Body | The Angels and Jinn |
| How to Pray Behind an Imām | Kindness and Forgiveness | Shaitān: The Invisible Enemy |
| **Unit 6: General Islamic Topics** | The Middle Path: Ways to Avoid Two Extremes | **Unit 7: The Current Soceity** |
| Compilers of Hadīth | Salāt: Its Significance | My Friend Is Muslim Now |
| Shaitān's Mode of Operation | Sawm: Its Significance | Friendship: How to Choose One |
| Day of Judgment | Zakāt and Sadaqah: Similarities and Differences | Muslims Around the World |
| Eid: Its Significance | | People of Other Faiths |
| Truthfulness: A Quality of Muslim | | **Unit 8: Developing Islamic Values** |
| Perseverance: Keep on Trying | | Greed and Dishonesty |
| | | Avoiding Extravagance |

# Outline of Curriculum – Levels 7, 8 and 9

In these levels, the application of knowledge is increasingly emphasized by offering carefully selected topics. Specific details about some of the messengers are introduced to highlight the abiding morals in their lives. In Level 8, early Muslim struggles are discussed in detail. Increased depth and information in the lessons require focused attention from students. Age-appropriate moral lessons are also covered including gossip, friendship, peer pressure, dating, indecency, encouraging good and forbidding evil.

| Level 7 | Level 8 | Level 9 |
| --- | --- | --- |
| **Unit 1: The Creator** | **Unit 1: Knowing the Creator** | **Unit 1: A Reflection on the Divine** |
| Why Islam? what is Islam? | Divine Names | Signs of Allāh in nature |
| Belief in Allāh | Sunan of Allāh | Pondering the Qur'ān |
| The Qur'ān: Its Qualitative Names | Objectives of the Qur'ān | Preservation and Compilation of the Qur'ān |
| Istighfar: Seeking Forgiveness of Allāh | Sūrah Hujurat: Its Teachings | Worship in Islam |
| Allāh: Angry or Kind | True Piety: Analysis of Verse 2:177 | **Unit 2: Islam and Muslims** |
| **Unit 2: Stories of the Messengers** | Ayātul Qursi | Why Human Beings Are Superior |
| Ādam (A): Trial of the Messenger | **Unit 2: The Messenger of Allāh** | Zulm—Wrongdoings |
| Life of Ibrāhīm (A) | The Person Muhammad | Is Islam a Violent Religion? |
| Sacrifice of Ibrāhīm (A) | Farewell Pilgrimage | Present Life—Vanity, Deception |
| Lūt (A): Message for Modern Societies | Finality of Prophethood | Shariah |
| Yūsuf (A)—The Will to Overcome Temptation | Hadīth: Collection, Classification | Justice in Islam |
| **Unit 3: Stories from the Qur'ān** | **Unit 3: Challenges in Madīnah** | **Unit 3: Ethical Standard in Islam** |
| Companions of the Cave | Hypocrites | Peer Pressure |
| Dhul Qurnain: Journey of a King | Banu Qaynuka | Choices We Make |
| Effective Debate and Negotiation Styles in the Qur'ān | Banu Nadir | Islamic Perspective on Dating |
| **Unit 4: Two Companions** | Banu Qurayzah | Indecency |
| Abū Sufyān | Mission to Tabūk | Alcohol and Gambling |
| Khālid Ibn Walīd (R) | **Unit 4: Islamic Ethical Framework** | Permitted and Prohibited Food |
| **Unit 5: Knowledge Enrichment** | Friends and Friendship | Food of the People of the Book |
| The Character of the Messengers | Friendship With Non-Muslims | **Unit 4: Essays on Rasulullāh** |
| Rasūlullāh's Marriages | Dating in Islam | Khadījah (ra) |
| Lailatul Qadr | Golden Rules to Live By | Rasūlullāh's Multiple Marriages |
| Fasting During Ramadan | Elements of Bad Life | Marriage to Zainab (ra) |
| My Family is Muslim Now | **Unit 5: Islamic Values, Teachings** | The Prophet: A Great Army General |
| Science in the Qur'ān | Duties Toward Parents | Prophecy of Muhammad in the Bible |
| Lessons from Past Civilizations | Hope, Hopefulness, Hopelessness | Allegations Against Rasūlullāh |
| **Unit 6: Teachings of the Qur'ān** | Trials in Life | **Unit 5: Towards a Better Islamic Life** |
| Amr Bil Ma'rūf | Permitted and Prohibited Food | Faith-Based Wealth Building |
| Guard Your Tongue | Performance of Hajj | Earning, Spending, Investing |
| Islamic Greetings | Parables in the Qur'ān | God's Chosen People |
| How to Achieve Success | **Unit 6: Islam After the Rasul (S)** | Fastest Growing Religion |
| Permitted and Prohibited | Origin and History of Shī'ah | Muslims in North America |
| Types of Behavior Allāh Loves | Ummayad Dynasty | |
| | Abbasid Dynasty | |

# Outline of Curriculum – Levels 10, 11–12

In Level 10 and 11–12, Islamic topics increasingly prepare youths to fine-tune their spiritual and social lives. Significant issues that have real-life implications are introduced. The application of knowledge continues to be emphasized. The lessons in the Level 11–12 book strongly promote the application of Islamic knowledge. This is achieved through carefully selected topics. All lessons teach core Islamic beliefs and understandings based on the Qur'ān and authentic Hadith.

| Level 10 | Level 11–12 |
|---|---|
| **Unit 1: Knowing the Creator** | **Unit 1: Understanding Our Belief** |
| Understanding the Word "Allāh" | Islam |
| Al-Fātihah: An Analysis of its Message | Muslim |
| Al-Fātihah vs The Lord's Prayer | Shahādah |
| Muhkam and Mutashābihat Āyāt | Belief in Allāh |
| Al-'Asr: The Formula of Success | Belief in the Angels |
| Qur'ānic Calligraphy | Belief in the Revealed Books |
| **Unit 2: Interfaith Studies** | Belief in the Messengers |
| The Bible and the Qur'ān | Belief in the Hereafter |
| The Ten Commandments and Islam | **Unit 2: The "Driver" Within Us** |
| Our Faiths: Key Differences | Life's Ultimate Purpose |
| **Unit 3: Marriage and Family in Islam** | Wealth Is The "Driver" |
| The Status of Women in Islam | The "Driver" Within Us |
| Marriage to Non-Muslims | **Unit 3: A Heart for Allāh** |
| Marrying Four Women | When Allāh Seems Distant |
| Difficult Questions on Marriage | Tawakkul: Trust in Allāh |
| A Muslim Family | Du'ā: How Does Allāh Respond? |
| **Unit 4: General Islamic Topics** | A Heart for Allāh |
| Who are the Khalīfah on Earth? | **Unit 4: Controlling Our Thoughts** |
| False Piety | Controlling Your Thoughts |
| Superstition | Maintaining a Relationship |
| Do Not Transgress Limits | The Power of Forgiveness |
| Secular and Religious Duties | Reading the Qur'ān |
| Islamic Views on Racism | Afraid to Think, Forbidden to Ask |
| **Unit 5: Principles of Finance in Islam** | **Unit 5: A Review of Key Concepts** |
| Public Finance in Early Islam | Lower Your Gaze |
| Wealth in The Qur'an | 'Ā'ishah (ra): The Child Bride |
| Islamic Investment | "Strike" in Sūrah An-Nisā' |
| Language of Investment | The Myth About the Satanic Verse |
| Faith-Based Wealth Building | How Jesus Became Christ |
| Managing Earning and spending | Rūh and Nafs |
| Leading an Interest Free Life | **Unit 6: Faith-Based Wealth Building** |
| **Unit 6: Islam and the World** | Taking financial control early |
| Islamic Architecture | Fundamental of Finance |
| Islam in Spain and Portugal | Islamic Investment |